BOWLING SECRETS
OF THE PROS

Bowling Secrets
of the Pros

• • •

EDITED BY
GEORGE SULLIVAN

Drawings by Dom Lupo

DOUBLEDAY & COMPANY, INC.
GARDEN CITY, NEW YORK

INTRODUCTION

This book presents a complete course in bowling instruction conducted by the world's leading professional stars. It is a genuine opportunity for the novice to learn the game and for the better-than-average bowler to increase his ability to score.

If you use this book properly, it cannot help but add pins to your average. But one word of warning is necessary. Not every bit of advice on these pages applies to every bowler. You must choose, putting into use only those pieces of counsel that apply to your style of delivery, even to your height and general build. For instance, not every bowler would be comfortable shooting from the outside, a suggestion of Roy Lown's. Few can master Lee Jouglard's three-step approach. In other words, the advice should be taken as mere suggestions, not stern dictates. Or, as any instructor tells his pupil, "Be natural; be yourself."

Professional bowling has gone through enormous changes in the past decade. In 1959 only three tournaments were presented by the Professional Bowlers Association, and the prize money they offered totaled no more than $47,000. In 1968, thirty-five tournaments, one of them at the new Madison Square Garden Center, were on the PBA schedule, and prize offerings had spiraled above $1,500,000.

With this type of money at stake each year, a prodigious amount of new young talent has been attracted to the sport. And because there is so much competition now, they reach bowling maturity very quickly. Through the 1950s, Don Carter, Dick Weber, Basil (Buzz) Fazio and Harry Smith dominated bowling. These stars are still on the scene, but now they must share billing with a score and more of new-comers, young men like Wayne Zahn, Dave Davis and Jim Stefanich.

It would be impossible to include all of bowling's "name" professionals in this book. From suggestions from bowling writers and industry officials, I have selected a cross section of them.

I am grateful to Dom Lupo, whose precise line drawings illustrate the text; to Ed Elias, founder and legal counsel of the PBA, for his help, and to Bud Fisher, PBA publicity director. Special thanks are due Glen Smallcomb for his cooperation, and Jack Moran for technical assistance. I am also grateful for the opportunity to consult past issues of *Bowling Magazine* and *The Bowler's Journal* in gathering biographical information on many of the bowlers this book features.

CONTENTS

1

THE BOWLING BALL

By Dave Soutar, WINNER, PBA NATIONAL

In November 1961, when lean and handsome Dave Soutar was twenty years old, he startled his colleagues on the pro bowling tour with a stunning victory in the PBA National, then the standout even on the tour. Since then, however, he has shown many times that this victory was more than blessed luck. Indeed, he has won rank as a splendid young bowler, and in 1967 he was one of the top ten leading money winners.

From Detroit, Dave won the Michigan State Junior Championships in 1959 and again in 1961, a year in which he also earned "Rookie of the Year" honors in the Detroit *Times* Classic. In 1962, 1963, and 1964 he was named "King of Detroit Bowlers," an outstanding honor considering the great quantity and high quality of bowler that represents the Motor City each year.

Soutar finished third in the 1964 World's Invitational. He won the Colorado Springs Open in 1965, and the same year teamed with Tom Harnisch of Tonawonda, New York, to win the BPAA National Doubles title. The pair edged out Dick Weber and Ray Bluth, perennial champions in the event.

Soutar's best series is 827, and he has also rolled an 804. He has six ABC-sanctioned 300 games. He is a member of the AMF Staff of Champions.

"The bowling ball shall have a circumference of not more than 27 inches." This, from the American Bowling Congress rulebook, is one of the specifications for the bowling ball, and it is about the only statement concerning the ball that does not stir hot debate. No one argues about the size of the ball. They haven't started to yet, at any rate. But such matters as the ball's weight, the size and pitch of the thumb and finger holes, the length of the span and the type of grip to be used are all highly controversial. This chapter will try to settle some of the debate.

How deeply you become involved in any of these assorted topics depends on whether you merely intend to borrow a "house ball" at your neighborhood bowling center or purchase a custom-fitted ball. If you're only going to borrow, your problems are slight. When it comes to purchasing a custom-fitted ball, the subject is a bit more complex, however.

Let's begin with the business of how one selects a house ball. The ball's weight is the first thing to consider. "The bowling ball shall weigh no more than 16 pounds," the ABC dictates. If every ball weighed sixteen pounds there would be no problem, but they range downward to nine pounds. What you must do is select the heaviest-weight ball that you can deliver while maintaining complete control of the ball. It stands to reason that a sixteen-pound ball will topple the most pins, but this only holds true if you are accurate with it, and you can't be accurate if the ball places any strain on your fingers or hand or impairs your smooth swing.

Most men pick out a sixteen-pound ball automatically. I think many of them feel it would reflect on their masculinity if they used anything less. But I'm convinced that a good percentage of the once-a-week bowlers would see their averages climb if they used a ball slightly less in weight than sixteen pounds, say fifteen pounds. Their accuracy would improve, I'm sure. They might pick up as much as one more spare per game, and to do that is to add ten pins to your score.

Finding a ball that is suitable in weight is largely a trial-and-error process. Try some practice rolls with a lightweight ball and work up to heavier-weight ones. Of course, a ball that is too light can be just as detrimental as one that is too heavy. With a ball that is not sufficient in weight, you'll have a tendency to rush the foul line. You are also likely to pull the ball to the left as you release.

Most women should use a ball in the twelve- to fifteen-pound range. Bowling balls for youngsters vary from nine to twelve pounds, although often a teen-age boy will use a fifteen- or sixteen-pounder. Lightweight spheres have cork centers, while a sixteen-pound ball is solid hard-rubber.

Just as important as the matter of weight is the subject of fit. The thumb hole and the finger holes must be the correct size. If they're not, all types of ills can develop.

Check out the thumb fit first. The thumb hole should be a bit roomy, yet not so large that you are able to double-up your thumb at all. Try this test: insert your thumb, then rotate it. The fit is right if you can feel just the slightest friction.

The fit of the fingers should be more snug than that of the thumb. Recall how the ball is released. In delivering a hook ball, the thumb must come out of the ball first, and then the fingers. It is the thumb that "unlocks" the grip, and that is why it must fit somewhat loosely. After the thumb releases, the fingers have to lift upward to impart roll to the ball and to give it direction. If the fit of the fingers is loose, they cannot perform in this way.

Another vital factor is span. This is the distance between the thumb and each of the finger holes as measured over the contour of the ball. If you use a ball with too wide a span it will be a great strain on your fingers, and you won't be able to keep firm control during the approach. Insert your thumb in the ball, and if you have to raise your thumb to insert your fingers, the span is too wide. If you use a ball in which the span is too narrow, you will find that you will be pinching the ball—that is, you will be doubling-up your thumb and your fingers in an effort to maintain your hold.

To tell if the span of your ball is right, insert your thumb. Then lay your fingers across the finger holes. The finger knuckles closest to your hand should go just beyond the inside edges of the finger holes.

The weight, the size of the thumb and finger holes, and the span—these are the three factors that have to be considered when you are selecting a house ball. Most bowling centers offer an extremely wide selection, and you are sure to find one that is satisfactory. When you do feel you have a ball that suits, stick with it. Don't switch because you have a bad game or two. Such changeableness is not likely to improve your performance. As long as the ball is comfortable and you have full control over it, you should be able to overcome any seeming deficiencies it might possess.

Make a note of the code number of the ball you choose. Most bowling centers have a reservation system, and the management will set aside the ball for you whenever you plan to bowl.

Any bowler really serious about his game will buy a custom-fitted ball. When you are planning to make such a purchase, be certain to consult an expert. Measuring a person for a ball and then drilling it out to conform to the measurements is an elaborate art.

Buy a quality ball, one put out by any one of the several leading bowling equipment manufacturers. You are then assured that the ball meets the exacting specifications of the American Bowling Congress. In recent years foreign-manufactured bowling balls, sold at discount prices, have begun to be marketed here. Sometimes these have a surface that is too brittle or too soft. A hard-surfaced ball tends to skid, while one with a surface that is soft quickly shows signs of wear. A quality bowling ball will give you years and years of use; an inferior one won't. So it simply isn't practical to go bargain-hunting when you are ready to purchase a bowling ball.

This does not mean you have to purchase the most expensive ball available. Not at all. Indeed, sometimes the most expensive balls owe their additional cost to such fancy features as eye-appealing color. The classic bowling ball, black and made of hard rubber (not plastic), which costs about twenty-five dollars, is the one I recommend.

One day I was in a bowling pro shop and a customer brought in a house ball, and said to the pro, "Here, drill me one just like it." This may seem a little foolish, but it's not—at least for the average bowler. After all, if you find a house ball that works well, the problems of weight and fit have been settled.

However, for the top-flight bowler this isn't enough. When a pro purchases a bowling ball, there are many other and quite technical particulars involved.

The pro knows what weight he wants—sixteen pounds—but his concern is with how that weight is distributed—in other words, how the ball is balanced. The American Bowling Congress recognizes that a bowling ball has six "sides." There is the top or finger hole side, and its opposing side, the bottom. Then there are the two opposing sides to the right and left of the finger holes, and the two other opposing sides to the front of the finger hole sides. Any one of these sides can be of greater weight than any of the others, and often a professional will specify a ball of this nature. There is a feeling that a ball so weighted drives into the pins with greater authority. Most stars choose a top-weighted ball, one where the concentration of weight is located near the finger holes.

This difference in weight concentration is not really great. In a ball that weighs ten pounds or more, the ABC specifies that the difference in weight concentration between the top and the bottom cannot be more than three ounces.

How do you determine top weight or side weight? Often the box in which a new ball is contained will be stamped with this information. Most bowling ball supply shops have a special scale—called a dodo scale—which can measure the amount of weight concentrated on any one of the sides. Of course, such concentrations of weight, when they do exist, have to have resulted from the manufacturing process. Side weight or top weight cannot be produced by placing any foreign material—a metal weight, for instance—on the surface of the ball.

After the professional has a ball that suits him, he takes it to a specialist who drills it according to the pro's specifications, or he may drill it himself. In ordering the grip he wants, the pro considers many factors, some of which the average bowler is not even aware of. Of course, the size of the thumb hole and finger holes is very important, but as far as the pro is concerned, this is a matter that has been long settled. The pro is much more interested in the style of his grip, and the placement and pitch of the holes. He will devote many hours to discussing and pondering these topics. Lou Campi, who twice shared the BPAA National Doubles title, spends from four to six months working over a new bowling ball until it suits his high standards exactly.

When you use a house ball, you do not choose the style of grip you want. All house balls have the same style. They have what is called a "conventional" grip. The ball has been drilled out so that the thumb can be inserted to its full length, and the span is such that it allows the fingers to be inserted to about three-quarters of their length. But very few professionals ever use a conventional grip. Instead they specify a semi-fingertip or a fingertip. Either one of these styles increases the bowler's ability to manipulate the ball at the time of release. This is what the pro bowler wants. With this style of grip, he can exert much greater lift and roll, and thus his ball will have increased power and drive.

The fingertip grip, sometimes called the full fingertip, is the more popular of these two styles by far. The thumb and the fingers are inserted only to the first joint. When the bowler takes hold of the ball, he is almost forced to clutch it, but he has enormous control at the time of release.

In the semi-fingertip style, often referred to as simply the "semi," the fingers are inserted to a point halfway between the first and second knuckles. Usually the thumb is inserted to full length. As you can judge, the semi is rather a compromise between the full fingertip and the conventional styles.

It must be said that not every bowler is successful with the fingertip or semi-fingertip styles of grip. Neither grip will produce high scores as a matter of course. You must have strong fingers and a quite powerful wrist. If you are not bowling at least three nights a week, do not consider using either the full fingertip or the semi.

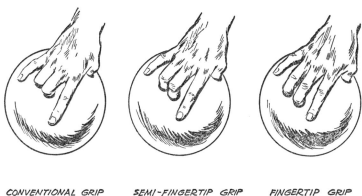

CONVENTIONAL GRIP   SEMI-FINGERTIP GRIP   FINGERTIP GRIP

Once the professional has decided upon the style of grip he wants, he must next determine how the thumb hole and finger holes are to be positioned in relation to each other. The next time you visit a bowling center examine a house ball and you will see that each of the finger holes is the same distance from the thumb hole. This is a neutral way of positioning. It makes it possible for the ball to be used by

both left-handed and right-handed bowlers. When you purchase a custom-fitted ball, however, the thumb hole is likely
to be placed nearer to the middle finger hole than to the hole
for the fourth finger (if you are right-handed). When the
holes are positioned in this way, they conform more exactly
to the configuration of your hand, and as a result you are
able to get a quicker release when you deliver the ball.

The professional bowler may or may not request this type
of positioning. Some specify that the thumb hole be set well
to the left of the hole for the middle finger. Others get a more
effective release when the positioning of the thumb hole
resembles that of the conventional grip. It is a critical topic,
yet there is a different opinion to match every hand configuration.

Besides the arrangement of the thumb hole and finger
holes, the professional must also specify the "pitch" of each.
Pitch is simply slant, the inward angle at which the holes
are bored into the ball. The direction in which the thumb
hole and finger holes are slanted is a key factor in how
easily you will be able to release the ball. How should your
ball be pitched? It is very much of an individual matter,
depending upon the size and form of your fingers and hand,
and how you deliver the ball. Consult an experienced ball-
drilling specialist for advice on this subject.

I will give you a few facts concerning pitch that may be
helpful as background. Pitch is expressed in inches, and it
is the distance at which an extended centerline of the drilled
hole passes above or below the center of the ball. If the
extended centerline of the drilled hole were to pass through
the center of the ball, it would be a case of zero or straight
pitch. If the centerline were to pass three-eighths of an inch
above the center, the hole would be defined as having three-
eighths inward pitch. If it were to pass three-eighths of an
inch below the center, it would be said to have three-eighths
reverse pitch. House balls are drilled with three-eighths in-

ward pitch on both the thumb and fingers, and this is the way your custom-drilled ball will be pitched unless you specify something different.

Pro bowlers realize that they can drastically vary the character of their release by regulating the way the holes are pitched. In the wide span grips that are common today, it is not unusual for the thumb hole to have an extreme reverse pitch. As a result the bowler can get his thumb out quickly and easily and this, of course, is what triggers the release. This is only one example. There are an infinite number of ways in which the holes may be pitched. Let me say again that the subject of pitch, like that of top weight and the style of the grip, are not matters the once- or twice-a-week bowler has to be concerned with.

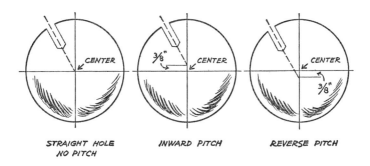

STRAIGHT HOLE
NO PITCH   INWARD PITCH   REVERSE PITCH

Nowadays, many bowlers question me as to the value of having special guides embedded in the ball. I'm sure you've seen them. They are usually white, circular, and a bit smaller than a dime in size. They are located near the holes. The merit of these guides are that they give you a good indication of how your ball is rolling, and if this information is of value to you, use them. A small piece of adhesive tape affixed to the ball will serve the same purpose, however.

Like any other piece of custom equipment, your bowling ball requires special care. Keep it clean. Buff it on one of the cleaning or polishing machines provided at the lanes, or rub it down with a cloth. But do this after you bowl, not before. In this way you avoid carrying lane dirt around in your bowling bag. Keeping your bag clean is the first step in keeping your ball clean.

Do not subject the ball to extremes of heat or cold. I once knew a bowler who used to keep his ball in the trunk of his car during the winter. One freezing cold night the ball split in half the first time he rolled it. This isn't likely to happen to you, but a ball that receives a severe chilling is likely to chip or crack. Extremely hot temperatures are also harmful. Never store a ball near a stove or radiator.

If you are not satisfied with the fit of your ball, you can have it plugged and redrilled. This is a fairly simple process and most bowling supply shops are equipped to do it. The holes of the ball are filled with a plastic substance which, when it hardens, is similar to the original substance out of which the ball is made. ABC rules make this mandatory. After the material hardens, the new holes are drilled.

Purchasing a bowling bag and bowling shoes shouldn't cause you the slightest bit of difficulty. Both of these equipment items are available in a wide range of prices and an impressive array of styles.

Summing Up

Use the heaviest-weight ball you can control. Men should roll a fifteen- or sixteen-pound ball, women a ball in the twelve- to fifteen-pound range, and youngsters a nine- to twelve-pounder.

The thumb hole should fit a bit on the loose side; the fit of the finger holes should be snugger.

The span—the distance between the thumb and each of the finger holes—is another important factor. Insert your thumb, and spread your fingers across the finger holes. If the span is right, the second knuckles of your fingers should go just beyond the inside edges of the finger holes.

Experienced bowlers use a fingertip or semi-fingertip grip to increase their ability of lift at release. In the fingertip, only the first knuckle of the fingers is inserted in the ball. In the semi-fingertip, the fingers are inserted to a point halfway between the first and second knuckles.

Take care of your ball. Keep it clean. Keep it out of extremes of heat and cold.

2

THE BOWLING LANE

By Pete Tountas, WINNER, TOLEDO OPEN

A native of Greece, Pete Tountas came to the United States in 1955 when he was thirteen. He began setting pins in a Hammond, Indiana, bowling center. "I started to bowl with some of the boys," he recalls. "Then I entered a league and averaged 195 the first season." He turned professional in 1962.

Pete finished fourth in the ABC Masters in 1963 and again in 1964. He compiled twenty-one four-game series above the 800 mark in Masters play, a feat the American Bowling Congress calls "one of bowling's greatest records."

His first PBA victory came in the Waukegan Open in 1964. He won the Toledo Open in 1966.

Pete finished second in the BPAA All Star in 1967. He was also runner-up in the PBA National at Madison Square Garden.

Pete's home is now in Tucson, Arizona. His highest series is an 827, and he also has an 801 to his credit. He has rolled one sanctioned 300 game.

I think one of the most marked differences between the amateur bowler and the professional is the attitude toward the bowling lane. To many an amateur the lane is merely a flat wooden surface which connects the approach and the pindeck (the area where the pins are set). But to the professional the lane is a great deal more. He realizes that lanes are like fingerprints—no two are alike, and each brings to bear its distinctive personality upon the roll of the ball.

Take the case of Dick Weber, surely one of the most

successful pros of recent years. There are many reasons why Dick has achieved a mastery of the game, but surely one of the foremost is his ability to adjust the roll of his ball to the type of lane on which he is bowling as he moves from city to city on the professional circuit. Dick says that only 20 per cent of the lanes are what he might call "normal." All the others require subtle changes in technique.

Before setting down some recommendations as to when to adjust your delivery, how, and how much, let's take a close-up look at the standard bowling lane. There are over one hundred thousand lanes in operation, and the American Bowling Congress lists these specifications for each of them:

Length: 62 feet, $10\frac{3}{16}$ inches, from the foul line to the pit; 60 feet from the foul line to the center of the No. 1 pin.

Width: 41½ inches.

Levelness: 40/1000 inch is the maximum tolerance permitted.

Each lane must be made of wood. Over the past two decades maple and pine have been used exclusively. Maple is used for the first twenty-five feet of the lane and for the pindeck. Pine, a softer wood which cannot absorb the punishment maple can, is used over the balance. The two are spliced together. Some bowlers use the splice area nearest the foul line as an aid in targeting, but it is really too far away to be much help in this regard.

Almost every bowler is familiar with the standard targets. There are two sets of them. The most popular is located at a point twelve to sixteen feet beyond the foul line and consists of seven small triangles arranged in a triangular pattern. Often these are called rangefinders, but they are also known as targets, darts, diamonds, triangles, and target guide indicators. It doesn't matter what you call them, just be certain that you use them. They are indispensable when spot bowling (see Chapter 14).

A second set of targets, consisting of ten small, circular dowels, is embedded in the lane parallel to the foul line and six to eight feet beyond it. These, too, are used by the spot bowler, though not as frequently as the triangles.

After the lane has been built and the dowels and triangles set in place, it is sanded and resanded until it is brought to within ABC specifications for levelness. Each year the ABC carefully inspects each bowling lane in the country. If a lane does not meet specifications, it must be worked on until it does. Otherwise the bowling center will not be granted ABC sanction. This, of course, is vital to the conduct of league play.

After a new lane is brought to the proper degree of levelness, it is given several coats of an extremely hard, quick-drying lacquer. In the days before World War II, alleys were finished with coats of shellac. Compared to the lacquer used today, shellac was soft, and bowlers using a shellac-coated lane would wear a path—virtually a channel—in the finish from the foul line to the 1-3 pocket. The trick was to get your ball in this track when you bowled. When you did you couldn't help but score well. But the lacquer finishes used today keep the alley mirror-smooth. There is no track to speak of.

That's not the whole story by any means. Over the lacquer the bowling proprietor sprays on an oily finish, usually starting several feet in front of the headpin and continuing to within several feet of the foul line. Then this thin coat of oil is polished with a rotary buffer. This is done every day, and done with meticulous care. Indeed, alley maintenance is a substantial though somewhat mysterious science. Each bowling proprietor has clear and set opinions on how he wants his lanes maintained, yet seldom do two bowling centers perform the chore in precisely the same manner.

In one bowling center you may find that your ball breaks into the pocket with the greatest consistency. But in a second bowling center, just a few blocks away from the first, you seldom strike, even though you roll the ball in the same way and even at the same target. You find your ball is either hooking too much or not hooking enough. Often this is because of the different ways in which the lanes are maintained. One bowling center may use more or less oil than another, or the lanes may be buffed to a greater or lesser degree.

Lanes on which the ball does not hook easily—that is, lanes which have more than a normal amount of oil—are referred to as "fast" lanes. The opposite, lanes on which the ball does hook easily, are termed "slow." "Natural" lanes are those on which the bowler can roll his normal ball and expect to get a strike.

There are many other factors which can render a lane fast or slow. The time of day an alley is "dressed" is significant. It is likely to be fast right after the oil is applied, becoming progressively slower as time passes. The amount of play a lane receives is another important factor. A lane that has been used for thirty or forty games will be slower than one that has experienced little action. The temperature and humidity, even the time of year, can affect the lane's condition. On a rainy summer afternoon you must expect an alley to be quite different from what it is during a midwinter freeze.

Whenever you go bowling you must seek to establish lane conditions right at the beginning. First test the approach, especially the area near the foul line where you slide. Practice your slide. Be sure the sole of your shoe isn't going to stick. Then practice bowl. Deliver your normal strike ball several times, making certain to roll over your strike ball spot. Don't be concerned about how many pins you topple. Simply keep a careful watch on the path the ball traces. After just a few rolls, you should have a good idea whether the lane is fast, slow, or normal. You can also learn something of existing conditions by watching other bowlers bowl.

You should acquire some piece of information about a lane each time you roll a ball. Did you ever notice how the scores in a professional tournament often get higher toward the end of the event? This is because the bowlers are improving their line on each alley, game by game. Some pros even keep a written description of each alley's characteristics, and refer to these before they bowl. In the average twenty-four-lane bowling center a pro will be able to get a near-perfect line on all but one or two alleys.

Suppose you discover that a lane is slow. How do you adjust? The standard method is to move your starting position on the approach slightly to the left of what is normal for you. Don't move it more than a board or two, however. Keep your same target, your same spot, that is. When you line up in this fashion, you will send the ball on a wider arc, delaying the ball's break. If the ball continues to hit high on the headpin, or to cross in front of it, move farther to the left.

On a fast lane, do just the opposite—move your starting position to the right. This puts the ball on a more direct line to the 1-3 pin pocket.

Occasionally you will encounter a lane so radically slow or fast that the mere adjustment of your starting position will not be enough to overcome the abnormal conditions. Even though you move far to the left on the approach, the lane is so dry your ball persists in coming in high. When this happens, try making an adjustment in the speed of your ball. For a slow lane the idea is to speed up the ball's roll. This reduces the amount of traction and the ball is not able to hook so much. On a fast lane, you slow the roll of the ball. This has the opposite effect—that is, it increases the adhesive friction of the ball, thereby increasing its ability to hook.

Never attempt to either speed up or retard your armswing in your efforts to control the speed of the ball. There's a much easier way. It's done with the pushaway and the pendulum swing. When you want to increase the ball's speed, hold it at a higher level as you take your stance. If it's normal for you to hold the ball at, say, waist level, position it at the level of your chest for more speed. Doing this will make the arc of your swing greater, and the ball will roll faster.

A third way to compensate for varying lane conditions is to move your spot to the right or left. Your starting position remains unchanged. Suppose your target is the second range-finder from the right-hand side of the lane. On a slow lane, your target would become the board just to the right of that. Instead of aiming at the tenth board from the right-hand side (the one in which the second rangefinder from the right is embedded), you would be aiming at the ninth board. This would delay the hooking action of the ball. On a fast lane, you would do the opposite—move your target to the left, to the eleventh board. Whenever conditions required, you would move two boards, not just one.

It must be said that adjusting one's targeting spot, or attempting to regulate the speed of the ball, are the less popular means of coping with lane conditions that are not quite normal. Most professionals simply prefer to move their starting position, moving left when they encounter a slow lane, right when they face a fast one.

When you take your practice rolls in your effort to determine the general conditions of the lane, you should also be on the lookout for trouble spots, areas that cause the ball to veer from its intended path. Even a very slight swerve can convert a potential strike ball into a split. A spot of alley oil that causes the ball to skid at a critical point is the type of thing I have in mind. Sometimes a lane will warp because of changes in humidity, causing a high board or a low board to present itself. Or sometimes the wood in a particular board will have an extremely wide grain (even though most alley builders try to discard such boards), and this can cause your ball to jump from its track.

When any such trouble spot appears, it can cause a real trial. About all that you can do is seek to bowl either outside or inside the problem area. You can adjust in any one of the ways mentioned above—by moving your stance position to the right or left, by regulating the ball's speed, or by changing your spot. It's tricky no matter how you try.

Imperfections in the bowling lane as those mentioned above are removed when the alley is resurfaced. This may be done as frequently as every other year. Resurfacing means that the lane is sanded from the foul line to the pit. All of the lacquer finish is stripped away and the lane is reduced to its raw condition. Then it is relacquered. If you bowl on a lane that has been resurfaced, one that has been well known to you in the past, you will find it has lost all of its former characteristics. It will be like a new lane, and you will have to begin learning the line all over again. You can expect a newly resurfaced lane to be very fast, too.

The approach area of the lane also deserves special consideration. The ABC specifies that the approach must be not less than fifteen feet in length, and permits a tolerance of ¼ inch in levelness. Maple is used in building the approach and it is treated with hard lacquer in much the same way the lane is.

Three sets of small circular dowels are embedded in the approach, and these are almost as important to the bowler as the lane rangefinders. There a maximum of seven dowels in each of the sets. They are arranged parallel to the foul line. One set is located two to six inches from the foul line; a second eleven to twelve feet from the line, and a third fourteen to fifteen feet from it.

Always use one set of the guides in finding your starting position before you roll. They help you to line up both horizontally and vertically.

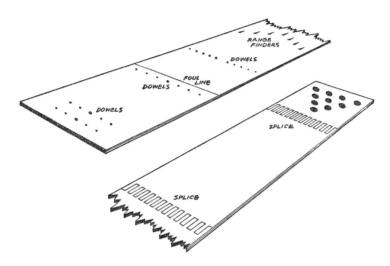

Use the dowels to assure that you are beginning your delivery at the correct distance from the foul line. Also use them to establish a correct right-to-left position. For instance, some bowlers place their left foot over the center dowel of one of the sets at the rear of the approach. They know that this will bring the ball in line with their target, the second rangefinder from the right-hand side.

The dowels can also serve as an efficient check as to whether you are approaching the foul line in a straight line— that is, not drifting to the right or left. If you begin your approach with your left foot over one of the center dowels at the rear of the approach, then your left foot should bear the same relationship to the center dowel of the foul line series at the conclusion of your delivery.

The approach part of the alley has to be maintained by the bowling center personnel in such a way that it offers you a good sliding surface, yet gives you enough traction so that it doesn't feel slippery. Usually this delicate balance is achieved by polishing the approach each day with a circular pad of steel wool mounted beneath a rotary buffer. Sometimes, however, despite careful maintenance, you will encounter an approach that does not present conditions requisite for good bowling. You may get too much slide; you may stick. Either way you're in a snarl.

Sometimes these conditions exist through no fault of the alley management. A spell of high humidity can cause stickiness on the approaches. On the other hand, cold, crisp weather increases the bowler's tendency to slide.

When you stick on an approach, first call the condition to the attention of the lane management. Sometimes one of the lane employees will hand buff the sliding area with a small piece of steel wool and this will correct the condition. Other times the fault may be the bowler's. The sole of his left shoe may have picked up some dirt that impedes his slide. Always inspect the soles of your bowling shoes before you step out on an approach. If the left sole doesn't look clean and smooth, buff it with a piece of steel wool. Usually this is available at the bowling center's control counter.

Never attempt to doctor the approach with powder or resin or any other such substance. This is in violation of ABC regulations, which say: "No one shall mark on or shall introduce in any part of the approach or lane any substance which will have a tendency to injure, disfigure or place the approach in such condition as to detract from the possibility of other bowlers being able to take advantage of the usual conditions."

When you are confronted by an approach that is too slippery for you, try this: Take your car key and use the point of it to scuff up the sole of your sliding shoe. This should retard your slide.

Of course, you can exercise some degree of control over

your slide by regulating the bend of your left knee. The deeper you bend the knee, the greater your slide should be.

As every bowler knows, the foul line is what separates the approach from the lane. The ABC says the line must be ⅜ inch to one inch in width. You should realize that the foul line does not exist solely between the approach and the line, but actually stretches across the entire width of the bowling center, across the gutters, the ball return equipment, and the division boards. Any pins toppled when a foul is committed do not count, but the ball is to be counted as a ball bowled.

Today's bowling centers are equipped with automatic foul detection units. This device beams an electric eye above the foul line, and when you break the beam a Klaxon sounds and the automatic pinspotter resets the pins. When you go over the line, it is a foul whether or not the foul detector reports it. Sometimes the device may malfunction; other times it may not be turned on. Don't become careless in recording your fouls even though the detection equipment may be imperfect in reporting them. The best way to avoid foul penalties is to learn not to foul.

At instruction clinics I get many questions as to what constitutes a foul. One bowler asked me recently if he was guilty of a foul because his trouser cuff went over the line. Indeed this is a foul. The ABC regulations state that a foul occurs when "a part of the bowler's person encroaches upon or goes beyond the foul line and touches any part of the lane . . ." And a trouser cuff is a part of the bowler's person. So is the hem of a woman's skirt.

It is not a foul should your bowling ball roll over the foul line, even if it breaks the beam of the electric eye and sets off the buzzer. Your ball cannot commit a foul. Another case: No foul can be levied against the bowler who allows some object, such as a matchbook or a coin, to drop from his pocket beyond the foul line onto the lane.

Also, you must complete your delivery of the ball in order for a foul to be assessed. If you approach the foul line, cross it, but do not release the ball, it is a balk, but it is not a foul.

Besides the lane and the approach, there are several other items of equipment that have some measure of importance to you and your ability to score well. The side partitions between the alleys at the pit end—called kickbacks—play a part. They are covered by a fiber plate. In some bowling centers the kickback plates are treated with coats of hard lacquer to increase their liveliness and give the pins a greater rebound potential. The type of care and maintenance accorded the rear cushion, the gutter areas adjacent to the pindeck, and the pindeck itself also influence the amount of ricochet you can expect from the pins.

Then there are the pins themselves. In the days when bowling proprietors coated their lanes with shellac, pins were a great deal less cared for than they are today. In those days each pin was made from a solid block of wood; there was no plastic sheathing. When a pin showed signs of wear, it was smoothed down, sanded, and often the base was leveled off. This made the pin lighter in weight and even shorter, but bowlers seldom complained because such pins were easier to fell. Today it is much different, of course. Besides its coat of protecting white plastic, the present-day laminated maple pin is fitted with a tough plastic base. Thus excessive wear is prevented, and so is the possibility that a pin will be shaved down or sawed off.

As specified by the ABC, the bowling pin is 15 inches tall and approximately 4¾ inches in diameter at its widest point. The diameter at the base is 2¾ inches. Sometimes the pins in one bowling center may look taller and closer to you than they do in another. This is because of difference in the way the pins are lighted. Although this difference can be minute, often it is enough to affect your score. The

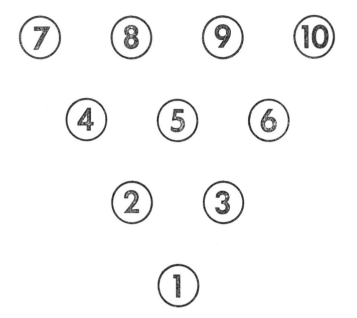

pins are set in a 36-inch triangle; it is 12 inches from the center of each pin "spot" to the center of the adjacent pin spot.

The ABC has established that pins must weigh as follows:

Solid wood and plastic coated pins	3 lbs., 2 ozs. to 3 lbs., 10 ozs.
Synthetic pins	3 lbs., 4 ozs. to 3 lbs., 6 ozs.

However, the weight of the individual pins within any set of ten cannot vary by any more than four ounces. Seldom does a bowler know what weight of pins he is rolling against, yet pin weight has a significant effect upon scores. Few bowlers do well against pins that are either particularly light or heavy. The ball sweeps right through the light wood without mixing it. The heavy wood isn't resilient enough to give you the necessary mix. The once-a-week bowler, that is, the one with an average between 150 and 160, usually achieves his best scores against medium-weight pins, those that weigh 3 lbs., 5 ozs. to 3 lbs., 6 ozs. The better bowler, because he rolls a stronger ball, requires pins that are an ounce or two heavier in order to do his best.

When you find yourself confronted by a set of pins that seems unduly light in weight, it is sometimes wise to move your starting position a board or two to the left. This will bring the ball into the pins on a wider arc and may provide you with increased mix. You can also try slowing the ball's speed. When you are facing heavy pins, do the opposite.

You should also be aware that the action of the pins can be significantly affected by temperature and humidity. The wood is much more resilient when the weather is cold and dry. Several years ago the ABC Tournament was held in Fort Worth, Texas. It opened late in the winter when the weather was wet and very humid, and it closed late in the spring following a prolonged dry spell. As a result almost all of the high scores were rolled in the tournament's final weeks because that's when the pins had the most bounce.

One word about one other piece of equipment—the automatic pinspotter. The machine works so efficiently that you probably are seldom aware of its existence. But occasionally the pinspotter presents the bowler with a situation that involves an interpretation of the rules. For instance, sometimes when the spotting table descends it unintentionally topples one or more pins. Such wood must be reset, with each pin being placed on its original pin spot. Another situation: in the case where a pinspotter sets the pins with one or more pins missing from the setup, the ball rolled must be declared a dead ball. A proper setup of pins must be spotted and then the ball bowled again.

From reading the paragraphs above, I hope you don't get the idea that the average bowler is confronted with one perplexing difficulty after another. The fact of the matter is that you can bowl for quite a stretch and never once encounter a sticky approach, a high board, heavy wood, or a pinspotter that malfunctions. But these problems occur enough to have some influence over your scores, and the more you bowl the more you will become aware of them. It's well to be prepared.

Summing Up

The lane targets consist of seven small triangles embedded in the lane at a point twelve to sixteen feet beyond the foul line, and a set of ten small circular dowels set in the lane parallel to the foul line and six to eight feet beyond it.

A lane that is "slow" causes the ball to hook more than normal. On a "fast" lane it is difficult to get the ball to hook.

To compensate for a slow lane, move your stance position slightly to the left; or increase the speed of the ball; or move your targeting spot a board or two to the right. On a fast lane, do the opposite.

Three sets of dowels are embedded in the approach, with a maximum of seven in each set. One set is located two to six inches from the foul line; a second set is eleven to twelve feet from the foul line, and a third set is fourteen to fifteen feet from the line. The dowels at the rear of the approach are to be used in determining your starting position. Those near the foul line are used to check your finishing position.

Never attempt to alter approach conditions with powder or any other substance. When you stick on the approach, buff the sole of your sliding shoe with a piece of steel wool. When you are sliding too much, scrape the sole with the point of a key.

A foul occurs whenever the bowler or "a part of the bowler's person encroaches upon or goes beyond the foul line and touches any part of the lane . . ." It is a foul whether or not the foul detector reports it.

Bowling pins must weigh from 3 lbs., 2 ozs. to 3 lbs., 10 ozs., and the weight of the individual pins within any set of ten cannot vary by more than 4 ozs. When bowling against pins that are unduly light in weight, move your stance position to the left to get a wider hook; slow the ball's speed. Against pins that are heavier than normal, do the opposite.

3

THE STANCE

By Butch Gearhart, Winner, Houston Open

Benjamin "Butch" Gearhart, a twenty-three-year-old left-hander from Fort Lauderdale, Florida, broke into the winner's circle on the PBA tour in 1967 in spectacular fashion, winning tournaments in both Oklahoma City and Houston. By the end of the summer tour, his earnings totaled almost fifteen thousand dollars.

Butch holds the ball about waist-high in his stance. "But don't bowl the way I do," Gearhart warns beginners. He angles his approach, cutting from right to left. "This is because I have an unorthodox 'pull swing,'" he explains. "Angling my approach is the only way I can get in back of the ball."

Sometimes it seems to me that there are almost as many types of stance as there are bowlers. When they take their starting positions, some people stand erect; others crouch. Some hoist the ball to shoulder level; others hold it close to the floor. There is nothing wrong with any one of these styles. In taking your stance, the key is to get into a comfortable and relaxed position, ready to concentrate on the approach and release, and you can go to almost any extreme you want to achieve this.

If you are a novice bowler, and unsure of just where to take your stance, try this: Stand with your back to the lane, your feet together, and your heels just touching the foul line. Take four natural walking steps (one for each step in your approach) and then a half step (for the slide). Turn around and face the pins. This is your point of origin; this is where you should take your stance on every roll. Make a mental note of where it is in relation to the dowels in the approach. If you are a three-step bowler, pace off 3½ steps. A five-step bowler should pace off 5½ steps.

How should the feet be positioned in the stance? It depends on how many steps in your approach. I use five steps, and thus my first step has to be taken with my left foot. When I take my stance, I place my right foot a few inches ahead of my left. This makes it completely natural for me to step off on my left foot. If you use a four-step style, you should position your right foot a few inches behind your left. This makes it natural for you to step off on your right.

Line up your left foot with a center dowel in the approach (no matter how many steps you take). This will bring the ball in line with the second rangefinder from the right-hand side, presumably your strike ball target. Point your toes straight ahead. Your weight should be equally distributed on both feet.

Your left hand should support most of the ball's weight. The fingers of your right hand should be held loosely in position in the finger holes. When you start forward, tighten your grip.

Most instructors recognize three basic types of stance positions. In the first, the bowler stands almost perfectly erect, and he holds the ball a few inches from his body and at about chin level. Shorter-than-average bowlers are likely to use this style.

The second type is the most common. The bowler bends slightly, his upper body leaning into the shot. The ball is held a few inches from his body and at waist level. You can't go very wrong if you set yourself this way.

The third style is a half crouch. The bowler bends from the waist and sinks in his knees slightly. The ball is positioned at waist level or a bit below. Because of the crouch, the ball is held out a greater distance from the body. This style is often used by bowlers who are taller than average, or anyone who has difficulty swinging the ball from a greater height. It makes for a shorter backswing.

At what level you hold the ball depends to some extent upon how much speed you want to achieve with your roll. If you don't have great natural speed, you will probably want to hold the ball fairly high in the stance, about the level of your chest. This means that when you execute your pushaway the ball will drop from a greater height than if you held it merely at waist level. As a result, it arcs into a higher backswing, and this, in turn, makes for increased speed on the lane.

Sometimes I adjust the level at which I hold the ball when I am faced with a difficult lane condition. For instance, when I encounter a lane that is running, that is, when the ball is hooking much more than is normal, and I want to speed up the ball's roll to cut down the size of my hook, I bring the ball to an even higher level than is normal for me. This serves to increase the speed of the ball and reduces the size of the hook. If I wanted to increase the size of my hook, I would do the opposite—hold the ball lower as I took my stance.

I don't recommend this strategy to everyone, however. When you adjust the level of the ball as you take your stance, you have to make a compensating adjustment in your footwork. If you hold the ball at a higher level than normal, then you have to take longer steps to keep in time. Attempting to do this can be a tricky piece of business.

In recent years many professional bowlers have developed the technique of holding the ball on the right side instead of directly in front of their body. A few actually hang the ball out to the right. This is a sound practice and the benefits it provides should be obvious. It's much easier to get the ball into its swing from a position on the right. On the first step of the approach, the ball does not have to be pushed to the right; it's already there. As a result there is much less likelihood of looping or sidearming the ball.

Ray Bluth of St. Louis, one of the most skilled of all the tournament pros for more than a decade, has one of bowling's most distinctive stances. He crouches, bends his knees, and holds the ball in his right hand, his grip hand. But the most unique part of his stance is that he raises the ball to a position in front of his face, and as he gets set to bowl he sights over the ball the way someone might aim down the barrel of a rifle. Bluth admits that this position is difficult to maintain and that it takes some time for him to get steady and balanced before he can begin his delivery. While this technique has worked well for Bluth, he doesn't recommend it to others. "Anyone who tries it does so at his own risk," he says.

Al Savas, a Milwaukee pro with nine ABC-sanctioned 300

games to his credit, is another bowler who owns a distinctive stance. Savas leans way over from the waist. His arms and hands hang down in front of him, and he supports the ball with his left hand. Savas executes no pushaway in the accepted sense because the ball is in the pendulum swing right from the start. With this type of stance, it's simple for him to achieve a to-and-fro swing that is perfectly straight.

Because of his deep bend, Savas is able to reach way out when he releases the ball. This helps him to lift. Naturally, this bit of unorthodoxy isn't recommended for the average bowler. But the styles of Savas and Bluth are evidence that the stance can be very much of your own making. The fundamental idea is to be comfortable and relaxed.

Once you take your stance position on the approach, but before you start to stride to the foul line, concentrate. Pick out your spot and focus your attention on it. Keep your eyes glued to the spot until your ball rolls over it.

Some pros spend long seconds in concentration. Others— Don Carter is one—seem hardly to pause at all. But every pro concentrates. It is the hallmark of the pro delivery.

Take plenty of time to find a stance that suits your height, build, and individual bowling style. Remember, it's the starting point for your approach and delivery. If it's not right, you can't expect to deliver an effective ball.

SUMMING UP

To find your point of origin, pace off 4½ steps from the foul line toward the rear of the approach (if you are a four-step bowler; a five-step bowler should pace off 5½ steps; a three-step bowler, 3½ steps).

If you step off with your right foot, place it a few inches in back of your left in the stance. If you step off with the left foot, do the opposite.

Line up your left foot with a center dowel in the approach. Point your toes straight ahead. Let your left hand support the weight of the ball.

There are three basic stance positions:

> *The upright stance:* the bowler is erect; the ball is at about chest level.

> *The bent stance:* the bowler leans into the shot; the ball is held about waist high.

> *The half crouch:* the bowler bends from the waist and sinks in the knees, and the ball is positioned at waist level or below.

The level at which you hold the ball helps to determine the speed which the ball will attain. For greater speed, hold the ball high.

Before you roll, pick out your spot; concentrate on it.

4

THE FOUR-STEP APPROACH

By Jim St. John, WORLD'S INVITATIONAL CHAMPION

Jim St. John skyrocketed to national prominence in 1963 when he won the World's Invitational Championship. While everyone else targeted in the conventional manner, he used an extreme outside line. The next year he did the same and won the tournament again. Many pros have since adopted the technique. Often it's referred to as "rolling the St. John line."

Jim St. John is one of the most respected competitors on the pro tour. In 1963 he won the Rockford Open, the Fort Smith, Arkansas, Open and the Meridian, Mississippi, Open. In 1964 he captured the Detroit Open.

St. John's record in team competition is just as glittering. In 1963, with the Falstaffs, he averaged 204 and the team won the BPAA national championship. The following year the squad won the ABC Classic competition. St. John boasts a 209 average in nine years of ABC competition.

In 1967 St. John pleased his hometown followers by winning the San Jose Open, a victory that included two games of 299 in the finals. He also won the Buckeye Open at Toledo that year, and finished high on the money winnings list.

St. John has rolled five ABC-sanctioned 300 games; his highest series is 807.

Sportswriters never fail to describe the pro tournament circuit as "grueling." Indeed it is. It can involve as many as a hundred games a week over almost forty weeks, and the conditions are completely different for each event. Because the season is so long and rugged, a pro has to get the ball to do as much work as possible. Anyone who tried to power the ball, that is, tried to force it into a high backswing and then tried to whip it forward wouldn't last through the first month. The trick is to simply allow the ball to go down, back and forward all by itself, to more or less just steer it.

I found out long ago that the ball is plenty heavy to knock over the pins by itself. It doesn't take muscle. High scores depend on a smooth and deliberate approach, and delivering the ball with accuracy. The key element in achieving this smoothness and deliberation is footwork, which the dictionary defines as "the manner of using the feet." I would say that footwork represents about 75 per cent of anyone's game.

You must plan a delivery that contains the correct number of steps, and each of them must be the correct length and executed with the proper tempo. Then it is a matter of co-ordinating your footwork with the rest of your delivery. In other words, your approach and release have to be carefully timed. When you are "in time" you will be able to deliver the ball easily and naturally. You will never have to force the ball to do anything.

As to the number of steps, I recommend four, no more and no less. Four. The four-step delivery gives you just the right amount of momentum you need to roll an effective ball. It helps you to achieve precise timing because the ball and your feet go into motion at the same time. Were you to use a five-step approach, you would find it necessary to take a preliminary step before the ball starts moving. This can be awkward. As for the three-step delivery, I look upon it as a "hurry-up-and-bowl" style. There's no pushaway; you don't have time for one. You really have to "muscle" the ball to get it to the foul line. If you are a beginner in bowling, be certain to try the four-step style before any other.

The first step is with the right foot. Then it's left, right, left—slide. If you are a person who finds it somewhat awkward to step out on the right foot, try this: When you take your stance, position your right foot slightly in back of your left. Then when you lean forward into your approach, you will instinctively move your right foot first. Try it at home. Stand with one foot beside the other, but with the toe of your right foot near the arch of your left. Now lean forward. Notice how your right foot and leg strain to move ahead.

The most critical phase of your approach occurs right at the beginning. As you step out with your right foot, you must push the ball away from your body. These two actions have to be performed simultaneously. If you perform them in the correct way, your troubles throughout the entire approach will be minimal, but make a mistake here and any number of things can go awry.

The first step is the most critical one of all. Do not lunge forward as if you were trying to crash through Green Bay's right tackle. Be slow and deliberate. Do not take a long step. One that is a bit shorter than a natural walking step will do.

When you push the ball out from your body, push it to the right (so it can swing past your hip) and in a slightly downward direction. This is called the pushaway, and if you execute this phase smoothly and rhythmically, you will scarcely notice the weight of the ball.

When you are in your stance position, the weight of the ball should rest in your left hand. But as you execute the pushaway, the weight of the ball gradually shifts to your right hand. As the pushaway nears completion, your left hand should not be on the ball at all. Remember to push the ball out to the full length of your right arm.

On the second step of the four-step delivery the ball, from

its position out in front of your body, goes into the swing. The step itself should be a little longer and a little bit more hurried. At the time you take the step, move your left arm out to counterbalance the weight of the ball. You do not have to force the ball into the swing. Simply let gravity take over. Gravity will swing the ball and your arm down and back into a smooth, unhurried arc.

As you execute your third step, the ball swings back from a position beside your right leg to the peak of the backswing. How high should the ball go? Certainly never above the level of your shoulders. However, let it swing naturally and it will find its own level. Don't force it back; don't stifle the swing. Keep your arm perfectly straight.

As you begin your fourth and final step, bring the ball forward. Your knees should be bent so that you are low to the lane. It is at this point in the delivery that many bowlers make the fatal mistake of lowering their right shoulder in an effort to get a smooth release. But if you have sufficient bend in your knees, especially the left knee, you will get a smooth release, and you are likely to keep your shoulders level.

Push forward on the ball of your left foot to get plenty of slide. Your toe should stop three or four inches from the foul line. Keep your body bent forward.

As you slide, your right arm should carry the ball over the line. Your thumb should come out of the ball first, and then your fingers. Lift with your fingers. The ball should never thud onto the lane. I try to visualize it as an airplane making a low approach to a landing strip and setting down gently.

It's vital to keep your head still and your eyes on your target. If you raise your head, or let your eyes stray to the right or left, even for a fraction of a second, it will adversely affect your release.

I bring my right arm into an extremely high follow-through, way above the head. I don't know exactly how I developed this exaggerated motion, but I've never bothered to change because it has produced the desired results—a smooth release and a hard-driving ball. But if your right hand comes only to the level of your shoulder in this final phase of the delivery, I'm sure it will be adequate. You should be so well balanced after your release that you can hold your follow-through position without wavering one bit.

Speed causes more approach and delivery problems than anything else. It absolutely wrecks your timing. Nevertheless, most young bowlers I see have almost a mania for "rushing the line." Thankfully, excessive speed has never been an acute problem for me. I think it's because I simply don't have the muscular strength to power the ball through the approach with flashing speed.

A good way to check whether your approach speed is correct is to look down at your left foot (your sliding foot) after you have sent the ball on its way. Your foot should be parallel to the boards in the approach; if it's turned to the right, it's almost certain you've rushed the line.

While your steps should be taken at about the same tempo as natural walking steps, it's an advantage if they gradually build in speed, with the first one being executed at the slowest rate, and the final step at the fastest. This acceleration helps you to get power and drive into the roll of the ball. Over-all, of course, your approach must be calm and deliberate.

Be sure you take your steps in a perfectly straight line. Any right or left drift will impair your accuracy. I know bowlers who are so determined to keep their steps in a straight line that in practice sessions they place short strips of masking tape on the approach to guide their feet. Try it. In total, a four-step approach should cover twelve feet or thereabouts.

Throughout your approach, your arm and wrist should be firm and rod-straight. Not tense, just firm. Most instructors compare the manner in which the arm swings to the way the pendulum swings on a grandfather's clock. The arm should go back and forth smoothly, without the hint of a hitch or a jerk. It should not deviate from its path by as much as a fraction of an inch. If you want to reduce the swing to the terms of physics, look at it this way. Your shoulder is the fulcrum, your arm is the lever, and the ball is the weight. Gravity controls the speed of the ball and the height of the swing—just as it does with the pendulum.

If you're a careful observer of televised bowling tournaments, you may realize that only a handful of professional bowlers use the four-step delivery, at least in its pure form.

Many use a five-step method, starting out on their left foot. In general, their steps are shorter and a bit more hurried.

The five-step style is remarkably similar to the four-step, however. The fifth step is really an extra step, one added at the beginning of the approach. In other words, the actions performed on the last four steps of the five-step delivery are precisely the same as those performed in the four-step delivery.

The extra step at the beginning is useful in achieving better timing and graceful rhythm. The ball hardly moves at all. It's on the second step (taken with the right foot) the ball reaches the peak of the backswing. The fifth step is a left-foot slide and the ball is brought forward for release.

A few bowlers do begin the pushaway with the first step of their five-step delivery. The ball then starts down on step two, continues into the backswing on three, reaches the peak of the backswing on four, and is brought forward and re-leased on five.

The reason that instructors shy away from teaching the five-step is because it increases your chances of making a mistake. The ball is in motion for a longer period of time. It takes more than the average amount of coordination to be able to execute the five-step successfully.

One mistake that bowlers make with this method is taking steps that are too long. The first step should be very short; in fact, most bowlers take only a half step on the first stride. It's sort of a slow shuffle. The other steps are somewhat shorter than normal walking steps. If your steps are too long you'll find yourself struggling to keep from going over the foul line at the point of release.

You also have to be wary that you don't generate too much speed when you use the five-step approach. There's a greater possibility of increasing your speed to such a degree that you ruin your timing. Your left foot gets to the line before the ball's forward swing. Few people begin bowling using the five-step method. It's best to become an accomplished four-stepper first and then switch.

Once you have developed your approach style, be consistent in its use. Use the same approach and delivery no matter what lane conditions you encounter. Use it whether you are going for a strike or a spare. Never vary it in the slightest, not even when you are after the tricky 10 pin.

Remember that one important key to success is allowing the ball to do as much work as possible. Be as smooth as you possibly can. One bowler on the pro tour who bowls in an effortless way is Bud Horn. He's as smooth as silk. Watch him.

SUMMING UP

The four-step delivery begins with the right foot; then it's left, right, left-slide. This sequence of action must be followed:

> First step—push the ball out, down, and to the right.
> Second step—let the ball swing down and back.
> Third step—the ball should reach the peak of the backswing; it should not go higher than the level of your shoulders.
> Fourth step—bring the ball forward; bend low to the lane; slide.

Set the ball down upon the lane gently. Follow through.

Strive for consistency.

The five-step delivery is similar to the four-step. The chief difference is the addition of a short timing step at the beginning of the approach.

5

THE THREE-STEP APPROACH

By *Lee Jouglard*, ALL-TIME ABC SINGLES CHAMPION

In 1944, when Lee Jouglard was twenty-three, he was introduced to the All Star bowling champion of the day. "Son," the champ said, "You'll never become a top bowler with that three-step approach." Lee grinned—and went on to become one of bowling's ranking stars.

Lee was introduced to bowling on his twentieth birthday and used a three-step approach right from the beginning. "It wasn't very smooth at first," Lee recalls. "I did kind of a hop, step, and jump." But within three months Lee was bowling championship-size scores.

The year 1951 is an unforgettable one in Lee's career. He won the ABC Masters Championship (with a twenty-one-game average of 201) and fired a stunning 775 in the singles competition of the ABC Tournament, establishing a record that still stands. In the millions upon millions of games that have been rolled in the ABC event since, 775 has been topped only twice, both times in doubles competition. Lee—naturally—was elected Bowler of the Year in 1951.

Besides achieving standout individual success, Lee has proven to be an accomplished team bowler. During the 1950s he was anchor-man for the famed Stroh's team of Detroit, one of the most powerful aggregations ever assembled. In 1951 the team won the ABC All Events competition with a 9506. Lee's contribution was an impressive 2000. The team high, it earned him the Frank L. Pasdeloup trophy. Stroh's holds the all-time record for total pinfall in ten consecutive ABC Tournaments with 30,442 pins felled in the years 1950 through 1959. In six consecutive tournaments beginning in 1953, Lee averaged a splendid 204.

Lee is also noted for his talents as a bowling instructor. He has conducted bowling clinics in every section of the country, and he was the featured instructor on TV's "Bowling Stars."

Lee is a Californian. He was born in Oxnard and now makes his home in San Diego.

I must admit that there are very few bowling instructors who teach the three-step style of delivery. I'm not particularly happy about this, yet I can't disagree with the view that the four- or five-step methods of delivery are superior in almost every case.

By way of explanation, when you use the three-step style, you take your first step with your left foot, the second step with the right, and last comes a left-foot slide. It's all done very quickly, yet in that brief period the ball must go down, back, and then be brought forward, just as in the four- or five-step methods. This is what causes the trouble.

Only a very small number of three-steppers have achieved any degree of success in bowling. The late Ad Carlson was one, though his style was really more 2½ steps than three. Carlson "muscled" the ball to several tournament wins and achieved an outstanding record in ABC Tournament competition. He is a member of the Hall of Fame.

Then there was Coung Gengler, a fabulous character in bowling during the early 1900s. Gengler was a money bowler, and he toured the country—virtually the whole world, in fact—taking on all comers. He was not an authentic three-step bowler but he came close. He would stand a foot or two from the foul line, rock his body back and forth, then take one step and fire. In the early days of his career, Gengler rolled a palm ball—that is, a ball without any finger holes. But he had strong wrists and could put terrific spin on the ball.

Indeed, strength is a key factor any time you attempt a delivery that is less than four steps. Your arm has to be able to really speed the ball forward in the final stages of

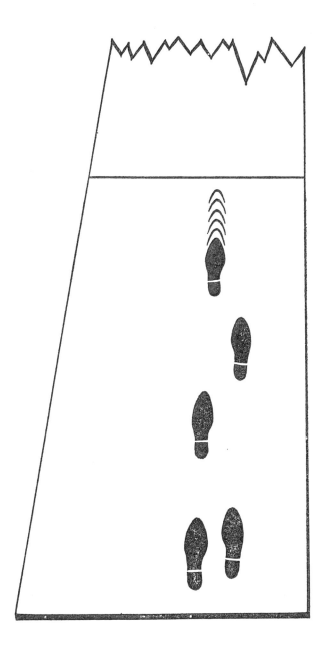

the approach. Otherwise your slide will be completed before
the ball is ready to be put on the lane.

As a youngster I was crazy about almost every sport, and
this is how I developed strong arms and shoulders. Baseball
was one of my favorite games; I was a pitcher. Horseshoe
pitching was the sport that probably helped me the most,
however. It built up the strength of my bowling hand and
arm and it also aided my rhythm and timing. When you
pitch horseshoes, you use a one-step delivery. You thrust
the shoe down into a backswing and then bring it forward
while you step ahead on your left foot. Once I started bowling
I found that it was relatively easy for me to get the ball
into the swing quickly and to pull it through on the final
step—the slide with the left foot. I simply duplicated much
of what I had been doing as a horseshoe pitcher, and thus
the three-step style was never any great problem to me. I
probably would have done all right with a two- or one-
step style, too.

Since the three-step bowler takes his stance closer to the
foul line, he usually uses the dowel series that is twelve feet
from the foul line in lining up. His stance should be fairly
erect. I position the ball at about waist level. Surely it can't
be positioned any higher than that. If you try to hold it
at, say, chest level you won't be able to get the ball swinging
quickly enough.

It is not possible to execute a conventional pushaway. If
you see a successful three-step bowler who does have a fully
developed pushaway, it's because he starts the ball moving
even before he takes his first step. When I take my first
step—with my left foot—I push the ball down to the right
and swing it back. Before the step is completed the ball is
well past my right side and into the backswing. Thus I
produce as much arm action on the first step of my approach
as the four-step bowler produces on his first two.

The average bowler finds doing this a bit awkward. Try

it. If you don't have a strong hand and arm, the ball will pull you off balance when you thrust it down. Most bowlers —women, in particular—must push the ball away from their body on the first step. They must push it straight out. Only in this way can they get a proper pendulum swing.

On the second step (with the right foot) the ball reaches the peak of the backswing. Your arm and wrist should be straight.

The third step is a slide and the ball is released. In this phase, too, superior arm strength is necessary. It takes a powerful arm to get the ball to the foul line because you do not generate enough body momentum to help the swing.

I recommend the conventional "shake hands" release, with the thumb pointing at ten or eleven o'clock and the fingers underneath and to the side of the ball. The ball has to be delivered well over the foul line, and the right hand and arm swing upward into the follow-through. As in any type of delivery—even in pitching horseshoes—you must bend your left knee to get down low. Your right foot is in back of you, helping you maintain your balance.

The ball rolls the same way in the three-step delivery as it does in the four-step. You play the same angles. A 1-3 pocket hit is likely to get you a strike; come in on the nose and you might leave the 7-10.

When I deliver a strike ball, my target is generally a board or two to the right or left of the second rangefinder from the right-hand side, depending upon conditions. Compared to the so-called "new breed" of professional, I roll a fairly wide hook. It breaks about six or seven boards. On spare shots I always pin bowl—go right for a target at the end of the lane. This is the way I learned to do it and I've never tried to change.

Sometimes a man who is taller than average can use the three-step style successfully. This is because the steps in his approach are longer and as a result he has enough time to put the ball into its proper swing. The three-step method is also a reasonable alternative for those people who lack the coordination necessary to execute an efficient four-step delivery.

Many people who have watched me bowl either on television or "live" have remarked to me how smooth my approach is. They try to copy me. I've been told that I make bowling look easy. But these people don't stop to realize that I have been using three steps for about twenty years. I really have it down pat.

I only recommend the three-step style in the cases I have mentioned above. When I'm instructing bowlers, however, and I see a man or a woman using three steps, I don't attempt to convert them to something else. I merely try to improve their delivery, usually helping them to get the ball into the armswing quicker.

When you use a four- or five-step delivery, you're able to approach the foul line calmly and deliberately. It's not too difficult to achieve really perfect timing. But with the three-step method an error in timing is much more likely. The three-step style is not exactly wrong, but it is not a simple way to bowl.

SUMMING UP

The first step of the three-step delivery is with the left foot. At the same time the ball must be pushed down and swung back. On the second step (with the right foot) the ball reaches the peak of the backswing. The third step is a slide and the ball is released.

Superior arm strength is required to be able to execute the three-step delivery successfully. It's necessary to thrust the ball down to the side on the first step without upsetting one's balance, and power the ball to the point of release on the final step.

6

SLIDE AND RELEASE

By Wayne Zahn, BOWLER OF THE YEAR, 1966

If there is any bowler that typifies bowling's "new breed" of champion, it is young Wayne Zahn of Atlanta, Georgia. In 1966, when he
was twenty-five years old, Zahn shot out the lights. He won the coveted
Tournament of Champions crown and later in the year captured the
PBA National Championship. He accrued almost fifty-five thousand
dollars in earnings and was named Bowler of the Year by both the
Bowling Writers Association of America and *The Sporting News.* As
if to prove his super season was no fluke, the following year—1967—
Zahn was again the average leader on the pro circuit, this time with a
213.5 mark.

It wasn't many years ago that Zahn had doubts whether he should
even try bowling as a career. He was a successful high school pitcher
and the St. Louis Cardinals and the San Francisco Giants felt he
could perform in the major leagues. "But I didn't look forward to
starting in one of baseball's low minor leagues," Zahn says. "Both my
dad and I felt I could make the top faster in bowling—if I was going
to make it in any sport."

In 1960, Zahn's rookie year on the pro circuit, he cashed very few
checks, and the following year saw little improvement. But 1963 was
different. He won his first pro title—the Chicago Open—and cashed in
in seventeen of twenty-six events. In 1964 he did even better, winning
the Buffalo (N.Y.) Open and the Northern California Open in Lodi.
He raised his earnings to $16,715, about two thousand dollars better
than the previous year.

Toward the end of 1964, Zahn went into a prolonged slump. "My
big hook caused me the trouble," he says. "When the lanes were
right for it, I'd do fine. But when the lanes hooked, too, I was in

trouble." Zahn worked on the problem for a solid month under the direction of Bill Bunetta, one of bowling's most noted instructors. The work paid rich dividends.

By the end of 1965, Zahn was showing marked improvement. And 1966 was the banner year. He won the twenty-five-thousand-dollar first prize in the Tournament of Champions, the most lucrative event on the PBA tour. He finished in the money in twelve of the next fourteen tournaments, including a victory in the Seattle Open. Then in November of that year he won the National Championships at Garden City, New York. The ten-thousand-dollar first prize raised his earnings to $54,650, breaking Don Carter's record by almost five thousand dollars. Besides his financial success, he scored an esthetic victory by winning the George Young trophy, given annually by the PBA to the pro who attains the highest average on the tour.

The same year Zahn finished third in the ABC Masters. He established a record in the qualifying round by toppling 1853 pins.

Zahn was born and brought up in Milwaukee. He led the Milwaukee Masters League with a 222 average in the 1960–61 season. He was only nineteen at the time.

His best series is an 802. He has three ABC-sanctioned 300 games. He is a member of AMF's Staff of Champions, and when not occupied with competitive bowling he conducts bowling instruction schools and clinics.

When the third step of your delivery has been completed, the ball is at the peak of the backswing, poised for delivery. This chapter concerns what happens next, the final phase of the approach—the forward swing of the ball, the slide, and the release.

While the general rule is that the backswing should never be any higher than the level of your shoulders, there is a growing trend among the better bowlers toward a shorter backswing, one that does not get any higher than waist level. This has been found to produce sufficient speed and power. It encourages less hook but more roll, and that is what most of today's professionals are seeking.

The shorter backswing is something to consider, but this is not to imply that you should put a tight rein on the ball's swing. Never do that. Too little backswing can be extremely harmful. It can force you to struggle with the ball to get it onto the lane. About all you will have to show for an evening of bowling is a sore shoulder. The ball should get well by the right leg and about to waist level.

The most common backswing fault is allowing the ball to go too high, above the level of the shoulders. Oddly, the bowlers who are guilty of excessive backswing the most are not heavy, muscular men, but petite women. They do it in an effort to roll a fast and powerful ball. Small and demure Mary Louise Young, one of Texas' outstanding women bowlers over the past decade, almost puts the ball into orbit in her backswing. It actually sails to a point almost directly above her head. Spectators have been known to take cover when Mary Louise is firing. While this style works well for her, it is likely to cause the average bowler serious problems. For one thing, it is extremely difficult— almost impossible—to keep the ball under control once it has arced high in the air. As a result your accuracy is certain to be impaired.

What happens is that the ball gets off the track. It loops behind your body, and to bring the ball back you have to sidearm. Many bowlers are guilty of sidearming and aren't even aware of it.

A good way to check if you are sidearming, or to break yourself of the sidearming habit, is to bowl with a folded score sheet under your arm. If you can deliver the ball without the score sheet falling to the floor, you can almost be certain you are keeping the ball on its proper to-and-fro path. But if the score sheet drops, the chances are very good that you are sidearming.

Quite often a high backswing can be a painful problem. Several years ago Dick Weber toured the Middle East for the State Department with other members of his bowling team. They had to bowl exhibition matches on lanes that received next to no maintenance, and Dick got into a high backswing habit, blazing the ball down the lane. When Dick returned to the United States, he found he couldn't rid himself of the practice. The situation became so serious that it actually threatened his career. Finally he reduced the length of his approach by about two feet, and this resulted in a slower delivery, shorter steps, and a lower backswing. But it took him almost a year before he resumed his winning ways.

The standard method of controlling the backswing's height is to keep the body fairly erect throughout the approach, or at least until the final step. When you bend low, you are forced to arc the ball high above the level of your shoulders. When I'm having problems with my backswing, I've found it necessary to have an instructor check my approach. He is better able to detect whether my backswing is too high or not high enough.

People who are short and stocky often have backswing troubles. This is because they have trouble getting the ball past their right hip. They put a loop into their swing as a result. This problem can usually be overcome in the stance simply by holding the ball well to the right, and then turning the shoulders slightly to the right before the ball is delivered. This serves to pull the right hip out of the way.

From the peak of the backswing, the bowler pushes into his foul line slide and releases the ball. This is bowling's "moment of truth." The ball passes from the bowler's control, and his role is reduced to that of a mere watcher as the ball begins its long journey to the pins.

There are two principal aspects to this final phase of the delivery: the slide and the release. Each one has to be executed perfectly.

As you come through to release the ball, your eyes should be fixed on your target. Your left arm is outstretched, counterbalancing the weight of the ball.

As your slide begins, your body should be bent at the waist, and your left knee should be bent, too. Only in this way can you achieve a slide. By bending your knee, you're able to keep the rubber heel from making contact with the approach and halting the slide. The knee bend also makes it easy for you to push forward on the ball of your left foot, and you must do this to get a good slide. When your toes come within two to six inches of the foul line, touch your heel to the floor to brake.

Some bowlers slide eighteen inches and even more. Buzz Fazio does this. But a slide that is eight to twelve inches in length should be sufficient.

The reason for the slide should be obvious. Without it you would not be able to attain a smooth release. If you stopped abruptly, the ball would jerk from your hand and thump onto the lane. All accuracy would be lost; power would vanish.

It is vital to bend low to the lane throughout this phase of the approach. I do not mean that you should merely stoop. Your whole body must get down low. Bend at the waist; lean into the shot. But bend the left knee, too; really bend it!

As your sliding foot approaches the foul line, your right arm continues forward. The toe of your sliding foot should reach the foul line at the same instant that you release the ball. Your thumb should be pointing at about ten o'clock and your fingers should be beneath the ball. This will give you a hook ball. Your wrist must be straight and firm.

You cannot allow the ball to merely roll off your fingers. You really have to grip. When the fingers lift, you must feel pressure upon them, even though it is only for a split second. Otherwise your ball won't work. Your thumb must come out of the ball first; your fingers follow. After your thumb releases, you will notice that most of the ball's weight

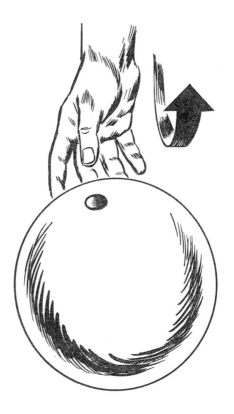

transfers to your middle finger. It's at this point that you must pull your hand upward.

The position of the thumb is critical. A ten-o'clock release is what is recommended. Allow your thumb to swing in a counterclockwise direction and notice what happens to the fingers. They are no longer beneath the ball; they are pointing downward. You could never roll a hook with your fingers in that position. Turn your thumb the opposite way—clockwise. Now the fingers are positioned in such a way that you are liable to roll a backup ball.

Occasionally you will see a bowler bring the ball to the foul line with his thumb set at a twelve- or even a one-o'clock position—far to the right—yet the ball he rolls is a sharp-breaking hook. How come? The trick has to do with the wrist. As he releases the ball, he turns his wrist to the left, bringing the thumb into a ten-o'clock position.

Why bother with this? Why not simply go by the "book." The answer has to do with the character of the hook. A bowler who gives his wrist a quick turn to the left, and combines this with a counterclockwise lift, will deliver a semi-spinner, a ball that rolls in such a way that a track will be circumscribed just outside the thumbhole. This is a much-favored type of ball among professionals. It is considered to be the most effective strikemaker.

The full roller is a second type of ball the pros seek. At the same time it is hooking, the ball is rolling over and over, like a stone rolls down a mountainside. To achieve this type of roll, the wrist has to be turned to the right at release. The thumb goes from a ten- to an eleven-o'clock position. The lift is in a counterclockwise direction, too.

As the ball leaves your hand it should be no more than an inch or two from the deck. It remains in the air for a split second, or only long enough to land a few inches beyond the foul line.

After the fingers lift, the right hand must sweep high into a high follow-through. Otherwise the lift will have little or no effect; you won't get your hook. Or the ball is liable to veer to the right or left.

The follow-through is simple. All your weight should be on your left foot, but lean into the direction the ball is going. Keep your right foot back to help you maintain your balance. Your left hand will go back—naturally. Sweep your right hand upward, at least as high as your shoulders. No part of the release or follow-through should be rushed, and you should be in such perfect balance that you can hold your follow-through position until the ball strikes the pins.

Remember, the arm's swing must be straight ahead. You

may have noticed that many of the pros angle their arm to the right as they release. The late Steve Nagy, a onetime BPAA National All Star champion, was noted for this. Nagy's normal style was to follow through in the accepted fashion, swinging the arm straight upward, but when he was rolling on a lane that was running, he would shoot his arm off to the right. His theory—and it worked—was that this variation dispelled his lift, reducing the ball's ability to hook. This isn't recommended to the amateur, however.

Keep your eyes fixed on your target as you follow through. "Keep your head down" is what golf professionals tell their pupils. It also holds true for bowling. Don't lift your eyes from your spot until the ball has rolled over it.

In the excitement of head-to-head competition, countless pros put an enormous amount of "body English" on the ball. But notice—they do this only after a full follow-through has been executed. Their foul line gyrations never interfere with their bowling form.

The slide, release, and follow-through are all completely natural. They are actions very similar to those in other participant sports. If you have skated, you will realize that bowling's foul line slide is very much like a skating stride. There should never be the least bit of awkwardness in your slide or release. If there is it's because you have a wrinkle that must be ironed out.

Summing Up

Never allow the ball in the backswing to arc higher than the level of your shoulders. In general, the shorter the backswing the better.

To control the backswing's height, keep fairly erect as you approach the foul line.

To get a smooth but forceful slide, push forward on the ball of your left foot. Touch your heel to the approach to brake. The slide should be eight to twelve inches in length.

To achieve a hook ball, position your thumb at ten o'clock as you release. Your fingers must be beneath the ball. Keep your wrist straight and firm. The ball should land just a few inches beyond the foul line.

After the fingers lift, swing your hand straight upward in a follow-through. Keep your eyes glued to your spot.

7

THE HOOK BALL

By Les Zikes, FIQ ALL EVENTS CHAMPION

Les Zikes is the first bowler in the history of the ABC Tournament to win three consecutive championships. In 1962 he paced his team with a 723 series to lead them to the team crown. He was a member of the team champions again in 1963 and 1964. And he won the all events crown himself in 1964 with a 2001 total. His fifteen-year average in the event is 198.

But it is in international competition that Les has fared his best. He captured the all events championship as a member of the first United States team to compete in the Fédération Internationale des Quilleurs' world tournament held in Mexico City in 1963. He fired a twenty-eight-game total of 5519. Les won the all events division of the FIQ Inter-Americas in Caracas, Venezuela, and the Tournament of the Americas in Miami in 1964. In the last-named event he boasted a 3942 for eighteen games. The same year he teamed with Jim Stefanich of Joliet, Illinois to win the doubles title in the FIQ Inter-Americas.

He also has excelled in international team competition. He was a member of the winning United States team in the FIQ world tournament held in Malmo, Sweden in 1967, and helped the United States eight-man team to victory with a 1610 for eight games.

Les's best series is a 750; his best ABC-sanctioned game is a 298.

A resident of Palatine, Illinois, he is manager of a bowling center in Arlington Heights, a Chicago suburb. He has his own bowling news program on Station WNWC in Arlington Heights.

The hook ball is the most effective delivery in bowling and every professional uses it. In a hook delivery, the ball travels straight down the lane until it reaches a point about fifteen feet from the pins; then it breaks sharply to the left and into the 1-3 pocket.

Why roll a hook? There are two basic reasons. First, because it is breaking sharply from right to left when it comes in contact with pins, the hook ball is not deflected as much as other types of delivery, specifically the curve ball or the straight ball. The hook powers its way through the standing pins to take out the 5 pin, the key pin in the setup.

The second reason the hook is so highly regarded has to do with the eggbeater effect it has upon the pins. It "mixes" the pins furiously. This is because in delivering a hook you must get the ball to roll, and roll is what causes mixing action. Roll is opposed to skid; a ball that skids won't mix the pins. It will slide right through them. Mixing action gives you a much wider target, and often all the pins will fall even though the ball is not squarely in the pocket.

Do not confuse the hook ball with the curve. The hook travels straight down the lane and then dives for the pins. The curve ball traces a long, lazy arc, first bending out and then bending back. Whereas the hook only crosses six or seven boards, a curve often crosses ten boards out and ten boards back, a total of twenty boards. This long journey causes the curve ball to lose its power and drive. It also exposes the ball to trouble spots that lurk in the lane. There is no lane that is really mirror smooth. What happens is that as the lane boards go through a normal drying process, they twist or bend. One board can become slightly higher or lower than the one adjacent to it. This is a booby trap. When your ball rolls over this area, it is nudged off course. From where you are standing you probably can't detect this happening, but when it does, the accuracy of your pitch is spoiled. The point is that the curve ball, because it travels over so many more boards than the hook, is much more likely to encounter one of these trouble spots. Develop a hook, not a curve.

One thing you should realize about the hook ball delivery is that it is completely natural. It is not necessary to employ any fancy tricks with your fingers or wrist as you release the ball. There is no magic to it at all. I have seen nine- and ten-year-old beginner bowlers roll devastating hooks, simply because they were so natural in their approach and delivery.

To determine your hand position for the hook ball release, stand with your hands at your side. Keep your wrist straight. Now lift your right hand as if you were going to shake hands with a friend. If you hold your hand in that position at the instant you release the ball, you will roll a hook of professional caliber. It's as simple as that.

If you want to be technical about it, your wrist should be positioned so that your thumb points at ten o'clock. Your fingers should be beneath the ball. Set your hand in this position when you take your stance, and hold it that way throughout the approach. You must also pay special attention to your wrist. Don't allow it to bend back, a common fault among beginners. Your hand and wrist should form a straight line to your elbow as you approach and release the ball.

At the instant of release, your thumb should come out of the ball first. Then let your fingers lift the ball. This lifting lasts only a split second. As you lift, your wrist will automatically turn in a counterclockwise direction. It's the lift that causes the ball to roll. As you release, the ball should be close to the deck, and it should stay in the air long enough to land a few inches beyond the foul line.

You'll see many bowlers purposefully turn their wrist to the left at the point of release in an effort to get a powerful hook. This is a mistake. Let your release be natural. If you turn your wrist to the left, you're liable to end up

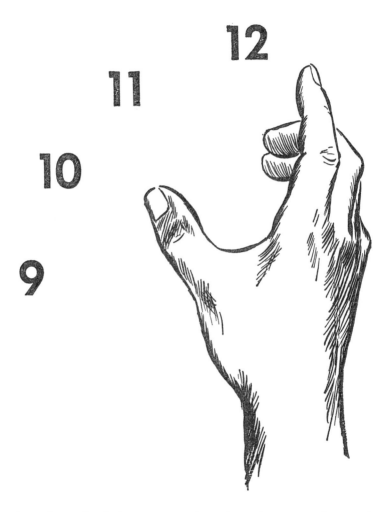

"topping" the ball. Instead of rolling, the ball will merely spin. There will be no hooking action, and no mixing action when it strikes the pins.

If you have ever been at a pro tournament or watched professional competition on television, you are probably aware that many of the top-flight stars perform some pretty unorthodox gyrations with the ball during the backswing phase of the approach. Bill Lillard, for instance, turns his wrist so his thumb is pointing away from his body at the peak of the backswing. On bringing the ball forward, he brings his thumb into a normal release position—about ten o'clock. Billy Welu and Don Ellis, Texans like Lillard, do this too. But this unique twist really isn't necessary to achieve a telling hook. It's best to keep your hand action as smooth and as natural as you can from stance to follow-through.

The size of your hook—the number of inches or boards that it breaks—really doesn't have too much significance. Remember, the reason for the hook is to make the ball roll, and to get plenty of mixing action. A small hook that breaks squarely into the pocket is every bit as effective as a wide-breaking ball, and it is a great deal easier to control.

There are figures to document this. On a strike ball delivery, the average bowler targets on the second rangefinder from the right-hand side of the lane. This particular rangefinder is imbedded in the tenth board from the right. Some technical expert has discovered that the bowler's greatest chance for a strike occurs when the ball enters the 1-3 pocket at the seventeenth board from the right, which means the ball needs to break over only seven boards, about seven inches. But wait. On the pro tour I have seen bowlers use the third rangefinder from the right as their target when going for a strike. This rangefinder is set in the fifteenth board from the right side. This means a number of the pros have a ball that breaks only two boards, about two inches! It should be clear—the size of the hook is of little consequence. Ball roll is what counts.

Timing and speed are two factors which have a great deal to do with the character and quality of the hook ball you deliver. Your timing has to be perfect. This means your left-foot slide and the release of the ball have to be performed simultaneously. Then your body will be poised and in perfect balance to execute the follow-through.

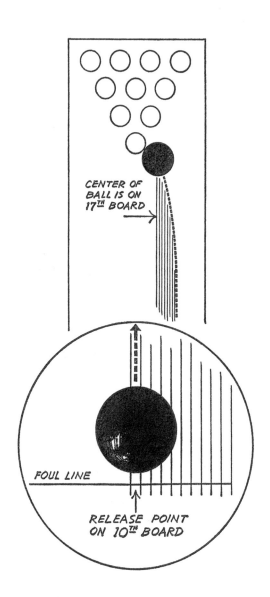

CENTER OF
BALL IS ON
17TH BOARD

FOUL LINE

RELEASE POINT
ON 10TH BOARD

Bowlers impair their timing with footwork that is too fast. They "rush" the foul line, and in so doing get ahead of the ball. This means they have to hurry their arm action to get the ball on the lane, and this often causes them to "dump" the ball (release it on the approach side of the foul line). If you don't believe that this happens frequently, simply check the approach area of a lane near the foul line. Notice all the black smudges. Each one has been caused by a bowler who rushed the line.

Of course, an approach that is too slow is just as harmful as one that is too fast. If you are too deliberate with your steps, you are likely to be pulled off balance by the weight of the ball. In addition, you won't be able to execute a foul line slide on your final step, and thus won't be able to achieve smoothness and accuracy with your release.

When your timing is right, you will know it. You will hardly notice the weight of the ball as you approach, and you will be in perfect balance at the time of release. The ball will have a splendid roll, and "walk" squarely into the 1-3 pocket.

Once you've learned to roll a hook ball, you next should teach yourself how to vary it from right to left. All alleys differ. Some are "slow," and the ball hooks readily. Some are "fast," and it's difficult to get even a slight ripple. Alleys not only vary in character from bowling center to bowling center, but even within individual centers. I once bowled in a center that had a radiator built into one of the side walls. The lanes closest to that wall, because they dried out, were invariably slow. The farther you bowled from the radiator, the faster the lanes became.

On a fast lane, with your ball failing to come up into the 1-3 pocket, move your starting position a bit to the right. Don't change your target. This procedure doesn't alter the size of your hook; instead, it puts your ball on a more direct line to the strike pocket. Move only a board or two at first. If the ball still doesn't reach the pocket, keep moving right.

On a slow lane, one where the ball hooks too much, do the opposite—move to the left. This will cause the ball to hook later. Keep your same target.

This type of adjusting almost always works with success. Sometimes, however, you may be confronted with lanes that are radically fast or slow, and changing your starting position won't produce the effect you're seeking. You may have to vary the speed of the ball. Increasing the speed of the ball will reduce the size of the ball's break.

I hesitate to recommend this system because it is a perilous one, leading to assorted problems in timing. To regulate the speed of the ball, you must adjust the height of your backswing. If you want a faster ball, arc the ball higher as it swings back. But you also have to make a compensating adjustment in your footwork. Because your backswing is higher, you have to slow your steps (or take longer ones) to keep in time.

This may sound quite complicated, and it is. That's why I advise you to keep to your natural delivery as long as you can. Changing speed should only be tried when everything else has failed.

I would be remiss if I did not mention the straight ball. Even though it does not have the devastating power of the hook, never underestimate its value. It is easy to learn, a cinch to control and, since it travels an arrow-straight path to the pins, makes the whole business of targeting much less complex. I recommend the straight ball to most beginners I instruct, and I also think it has merit for some experienced bowlers.

The principal disadvantage of the straight ball is that it has little spin, therefore less drive. It rolls over and over like a snowball going downhill, whereas a hook ball rolls, but it spins, too. And the straight ball does not angle into the 1-3 pocket like the hook; it hits straight-on. Thus it is easily turned aside by the pins. You can compensate for this somewhat by delivering the ball from the extreme right-hand side of the approach, almost as if you were trying for a spare on the left half of the lane. Aim the ball so it comes in fairly high on the 1 pin. In this way you get some right-to-left angle and reduce the amount of deflection.

As for your hand position, turn your wrist so that your thumb is on top of the ball, at twelve o'clock. Your fingers should be beneath the ball. As you release, the thumb hole of the ball should be on a direct line with your target. The thumb and fingers come out of the ball almost simultaneously. No spin is imparted by the fingers.

Do not try to roll the straight ball at too great a rate of speed. Since it is not spinning, it will knife right through the pins, toppling only those it actually hits. In other words, there will be little if any mix. You'll find that the straight ball produces the best results when it is delivered at medium speed.

I recommend the straight ball without hesitation to beginner bowlers. Since it involves a simpler delivery than the hook, it enables the novice to concentrate on his footwork and timing and other vital facets of the game. When he is accomplished in these, he can switch to the hook. Some bowlers never make the change; they stick with the straight ball. There is nothing wrong with this. You can develop amazing accuracy with the straight ball, and become a spare shooter par excellence. Of course, the hook ball gives the most dazzling results.

Besides the hook, the curve, and the straight ball, bowlers recognize one other type of delivery—the backup ball. Sometimes it is called a reverse hook, for it is a hook that travels the wrong way, from left to right. The backup is extremely difficult to control and produces no mix when it strikes the pins. It should definitely be avoided.

Despite all of its drawbacks, you do see the backup style in use from time to time. I think it is because most people using the backup don't know how to switch to anything else. It's surely not because of the success they're having.

The backup ball almost always results from a lack of wrist control. The bowler is "loose-wristed," and he allows his thumb to swing around to a one- or two-o'clock position as the ball is released. His fingers get so far beneath the ball that they are actually to the left of center. As a result, when the ball is released the fingers impart a clockwise spin to the ball, and it hooks or curves from left to right. Sometimes straight ball bowlers fall into the backup habit simply by letting their thumb fall to the right at the time of release.

To overcome a backup delivery, you must concentrate on keeping your wrist in firm control. Slow your approach. After you've delivered the ball, check your thumb position. It should be between ten o'clock and twelve o'clock. It should never go beyond in either direction.

A backup delivery can also be caused by a poorly fitted ball. If the thumb hole of your ball is too tight, it can cause the ball to fade to the right after it is released. But this is an exception. Usually it is the bowler himself who is at fault.

Summing Up

To roll a hook ball, position your hand with your thumb pointing at ten o'clock. At the instant of release, let your thumb come out of the ball first. Lift with your fingers.

To get the ball to break more to the right, adjust your starting position to the right of what is normal for you. To cut down on the amount of your hook, move left. Adjust the speed of your ball only as a last resort.

To deliver a straight ball, turn your wrist so that your thumb is in a twelve-o'clock position on the ball. Your fingers should be beneath the ball. As you release, your thumb and fingers should come out of the ball simultaneously. Deliver the ball from the right side of the approach to get the maximum degree of angle and to reduce the amount of deflection.

To overcome a backup delivery, assure that your thumb does not fall to the right, that is, turn in a clockwise direction, beyond a twelve-o'clock position.

8

TARGETING

By Tom Harnisch, NATIONAL DOUBLES CHAMPION

Tall, good-looking Tom Harnisch, a regular on the pro circuit and a sometime winner, holds one vivid memory, not of a victory, but of a defeat. In the 1966 Tournament of Champions in Akron, Ohio, with a twenty-five-thousand-dollar first prize at stake, Harnisch was one frame away from a victory over Dave Davis in the semi-finals when he drew a 6-7 split. "That ball cost me at least nine thousand dollars, or as much as twenty-one thousand dollars," Tom recalls. "I finished fourth and had to settle for $3125."

But rather than shatter his confidence, the disappointment strengthened it. "It just wasn't meant to be," Tom says. He has no doubt that the next time he is confronted with a similar situation the outcome will be vastly different.

Tom began bowling when he was twelve, and by the time he was fifteen he was bowling in the best leagues in Buffalo, New York, near his hometown of Tonawonda. He received his seasoning as a professional by virtue of three years—1958–61—with the Detroit Stroh's. In 1961 the squad finished second in the Classic Division team competition of the ABC Tournament.

In 1965, Tom teamed with Detroiter Dave Soutar to win the BPAA National Doubles title. He also won the Waukegan Open that year.

Tom's best series is a 796; his best game is a 296. When not on the tour, Tom gives private lessons.

Long debates have been held over which method of targeting is best. There are three techniques from which you

can choose. There is the "spot" technique, a system cur-
rently in favor among the top-flight bowlers, and there are
the "pin" and "line" methods.

If you have had two or three seasons of bowling experience, I advise that you try the spot method. This means that
instead of aiming at the pins, which are sixty feet away, you
aim at a much closer target, at a "spot" in the lane that is in

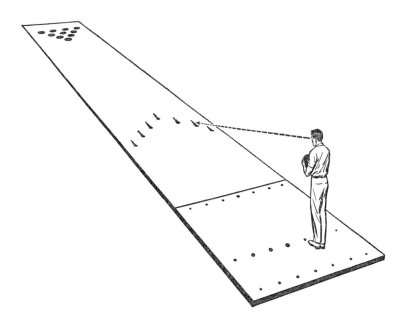

line with your target. If you choose the correct spot, and if
you hit it with a high degree of consistency, you'll find yourself stringing strikes.

It stands to reason that you cannot use the spot method
unless your roll of the ball is "grooved." Your approach and
release have to be so uniform that the ball you deliver
follows the same path time after time.

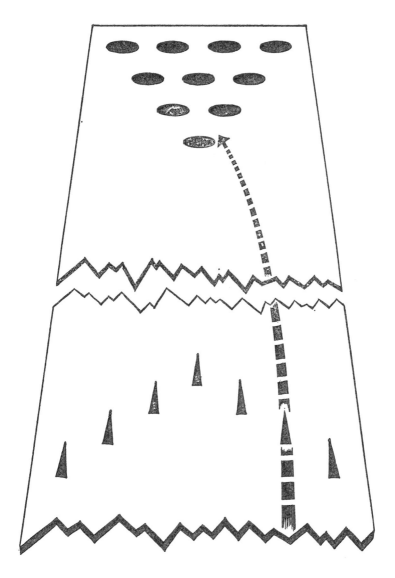

Most spot bowlers use the rangefinders in targeting. Beginners use the second rangefinder from the right-hand side
when shooting for strikes. If you take a careful look, you'll

notice that this rangefinder is ten boards in from the right-hand gutter. The 1-3 pocket is approximately eighteen boards in from the right-hand gutter. This means that if you roll your ball over the second rangefinder from the right, and it breaks at the correct instant, and its break covers eight boards, you will have a strike. Spot bowling is as scientific as that.

Some spot bowlers do not use the rangefinders for targeting because they simply aren't comfortable using this method. Some bowlers pick out a target nearer to the foul line. It can be any mark or mar upon the lane, or it can be one of the dowels in the string of ten imbedded in the lane at a distance of seven feet beyond the foul line. Use these if you wish, but don't bring your target very much closer. If you get too close, you'll find you must keep your head down in order to sight, and you're likely to arc the ball into too high a backswing as a result. Your target should be at least four feet beyond the foul line.

On the other hand, some people prefer to go beyond the rangefinders for their target. I know bowlers who pick out and aim for a specific board in the splice, the area where the lane maple and pine are joined, fifteen feet beyond the foul line. This target area is too far away for most people, however.

To find the spot that suits your delivery, roll your normal strike ball and carefully watch the path it traces to the pins. Does it roll over the second rangefinder from the right-hand side? If it does, then that can be your target. Perhaps, however, the ball rolls a board or two to the left or right of that rangefinder, in which case the particular board must serve as your spot.

Once you have determined a spot that suits your style of delivery, take care how you use it. Concentrate on the spot. Keep your eyes glued to it from the time you take your stance until you are well into your follow-through. I make it a practice never to lift my eyes from my spot until the ball has rolled over it. Follow this system and you shouldn't go wrong.

Of course, your spot won't be the same on every lane. When you're on a fast lane and your ball fails to hook as much as it does normally, you will have to adjust your spot. Move it to the left one board. If after a few practice rolls the ball still fails to come up into the pocket, move left another board. If the lane is slow—that is, if it causes your ball to hook excessively—move your spot to the right.

The paragraphs above outline the "pure" method of spot bowling. The bowler aims at only one target on the lane, and he never even glances at the pins. Many bowlers, however, use a variation of this system.

One modification calls for you to use two spots, not just one. One of these is usually a rangefinder, while the other is a point on the same board a few feet before or beyond the rangefinder. Bowlers using this variation of the spot system feel that it encourages them to line up properly.

While most of today's professionals use the spot system, and it is taught at bowling industry instruction schools and clinics, the pin method of targeting is still used by the greatest number of people. In the pin system, the bowler sets his sights on the 1-3 pocket and forgets everything else. I'm sure the reason more people use the pin system is because it's the instinctive way to bowl. If you were going to try to hit a tin can with a rock, you would look at the tin can and then fire the rock. Pin bowling is based on much the same premise. It may not be scientific, but it is altogether natural.

Pin bowling works well for many beginners. It is simple and it does not require great concentration. It also gives the bowler a greater margin for error. If you are spot bowling and you hurry your steps or speed up your armswing, your accuracy is going to be gravely affected. If you miss your spot on the lane by as little as a quarter of an inch, it can result in an 8-10 split instead of a strike. But when you pin bowl, mistakes in your approach and delivery are not quite so critical.

Line bowling is a combination of the pin and spot system. The bowler picks out a starting spot on the approach. Next he sights down the pins to the 1-3 pocket, and he draws an imaginary line from the pocket to his starting spot. The idea is to roll the ball along this line.

In using this technique, some bowlers target on a spot (on the lane) as they approach, but shift their eyes to the pins as the ball is released. Others do exactly the reverse; they concentrate on the pins as they approach, and then switch their gaze to a spot as the ball is released.

The various methods of targeting substantiate the fact that one's style of bowling is very much an individual matter. While the professionals use the spot method or one of its variations, not every bowler possesses the experience or temperament to handle it. My advice is to try the spot method first. If it works for you, fine; if it frustrates you, however, switch to one of the others. Keep experimenting until you find the targeting technique that produces the best results for you.

SUMMING UP

In spot bowling the idea is to roll the ball over a target that is near you on the lane, and that is in line with your target at the pins. Most beginners choose the second rangefinder from the right-hand side of the lane as their spot or target when rolling for a strike.

Pin bowling is a system of targeting in which the bowler aims directly for the 1-3 pocket. It is used mostly by bowling novices.

Line bowling is a combination of the spot and pin methods. The bowler rolls his ball along an imaginary line from a spot on the lane to the 1-3 pocket.

9

SPARE SHOOTING

By Basil (Buzz) Fazio, ABC MASTERS CHAMPION

Buzz Fazio, who celebrated his sixtieth birthday in 1968, is the only member of bowling's Hall of Fame still competing and still winning in tournament competition. When he isn't involved in bowling tournament play, Fazio sets his sights on the nearest golf course. He is a par shooter.

Fazio captained some of the most powerful teams in bowling history, including the "mighty Stroh's" of Detroit and the St. Louis Falstaffs. Both won ABC Tournament all-events championships, the Stroh's in 1951 and the Falstaff team in 1958.

Fazio has had few equals as a team leader and team bowler, but his individual accomplishments have also been outstanding. In 1955 he won the ABC Masters Tournament, and he has a 136-game average of 207 in Masters competition. Teamed with Tony Lindemann, Fazio won the BPAA doubles title in 1951 and 1954.

On the PBA tour, Fazio captured the New Jersey Open at Princeton in 1964, and accrued $18,470 in prize money for the year. In 1965 he won the Sacramento Open and a total of $15,685 in prize winnings.

Fazio has rolled two 800 series—814 and 802. He has four ABC-sanctioned 300 games to his credit.

The secret of successful spare shooting lies in selecting the correct starting position each time you bowl. From what I've observed, I would say that the failure to line up correctly causes well over half of all spare misses.

Always stand directly opposite the pins you're shooting

for. In other words, use as wide an angle as you possibly can. There is a good reason for doing this. When you position yourself opposite the pins left standing, you give your ball room to hook out and come back without tumbling into the gutter. You cannot topple the 10 pin by standing on the same side as the 10—the right side. Your ball simply wouldn't have enough room to hook.

Never use more than the width of the lane when taking your starting position. This can lead to difficulties. For example, when going for the 10 pin, more than a few bowlers stand well beyond the left edge of the lane. Some actually go as far as the approach area of the adjacent lane. But when they must bowl on a lane that has a ball return rack on the left-hand side, they have to keep within bounds, and this inhibits their approach.

To correctly line up for a spare shot, I recommend that you play one of three basic angles, what I call the 5, 7, or 10 pin angles. Use the 5 pin angle to convert spares in the center of lane, spares like the 1 pin, the 5, the 5-9, etc. As you take your stance, your left foot should be in the center of the approach.

For spares on the left half of the lane—the 4 pin, the 7, or any combination involving these pins—use the 7 pin angle. Stand on the right side of the approach.

For pins on the right half of the lane—the 10 or the 3-6-10, for instance—use the 10 pin angle. Take your stance on the left side of the approach.

Once you've determined your angle, point your body toward the pins. Look directly at them. Turn your shoulders. Last, look down at your feet to make certain you're going to walk a perfectly straight line in the direction of the target. When you set yourself in this fashion, you'll be better able to swing your arm in an arc that is parallel to your body. Thus, when you release the ball, you'll be able to reach for the pins smoothly and naturally. But if you don't face the

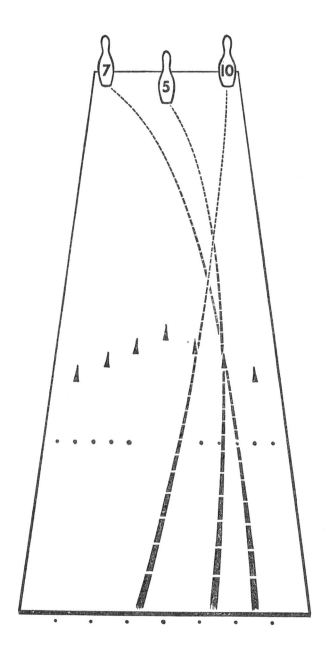

pins and then walk toward them, you are likely to find yourself making a desperate, last-minute attempt to get the ball on the right track. And when you try to "steer" the ball, you're in trouble.

I always roll my normal hook ball when going for spares. Most beginners don't do this. They feel they can't control their hook enough, so they have a tendency to roll more of a straight ball when going for spares. I think this is a mistake. It means you have to become accomplished in two distinctly different deliveries. Mastering just one is difficult enough. Stay with your hook ball delivery when trying for spares. Undoubtedly this plan will cost you some pins at first. But once you have a clear idea of how your hook behaves, you'll find the "single delivery" system best by far. Not only will you be successful as a spare shooter, but you'll find your strike ball percentage will be pleasingly high.

Two additional points are important in spare shooting. Always aim to hit the pin nearest to you, and always "cover" as many pins as you can with the ball. Follow these two pieces of advice and you'll find you can quickly determine your target on every spare setup.

For example, when you apply these two rules to the 3-6-10 spare, you know immediately that your target is in between the 3 and 6 pins, and you would not make the mistake of trying to carom the 3 pin into the 6, and then the 6 into the 10. The first rule tells you to topple the 3 pin. The second rule tells you to get as many other pins as you can with the ball. This can mean only the 6. Thus your target is in between the 3 and the 6.

In the 1-2-5 setup, your target would be in between the 1 pin and the 2 pin. In the 2-4-5-8 spare, your target would be the 2-5 pocket.

Once their target is established, many bowlers use a so-called "line" technique to hit it. They draw an imaginary line from their target at the pins to the foul line. Then they seek to roll the ball along this line. Other bowlers aim directly at the pins. They don't use any line or any spot. They seem to have an intuitive sense of where to place the ball.

Most professionals, however, and I am one of them, use one of the spot systems of targeting. I have tried them all and I feel that this one is the best.

My target on spares in the 7 pin range is the second arrow from the right-hand side of the lane. As I mentioned above, my starting position is opposite the pins—on the right side of the approach.

When I am trying for 5 pin or middle-of-the-lane spares, my target is exactly the same—the second arrow from the left. What changes, of course, is my starting position. Now my left foot is in the center of the approach.

When I'm attempting to convert pins in the 10 pin range, my target becomes the third arrow from the right-hand side. My starting position is on the left.

It must be said that these are only general recommendations. They are suited perfectly to the size of the hook ball I deliver, but they may not be suited to yours. Experiment. With just a few trial rolls you should be able to make whatever adjustments are necessary.

A word about single pin spares. Don't let them throw you. One good thing to bear in mind is that when you're shooting for a lone pin your target is of pretty substantial size, even if the pin is adjacent to the gutter, like the 7 or the 10. Look at it this way: the ball is 8½ inches in diameter; a pin, at its widest point, is 4¾ inches in diameter. In the case of the 7 or the 10, this means you have a target that is 13¼ inches. Don't make the mistake of believing you have to hit a bull's-eye the size of a dime.

If the single pin you're seeking to topple is in the middle of the alley—the 1 pin or the 5 pin—and you have a chance to hit it from either side as well as head on, your target area balloons in size. It becomes almost 22 inches (8½ inches plus 8½ inches plus 4¾ inches). Neither the 1 nor the 5 should ever be troublesome to you.

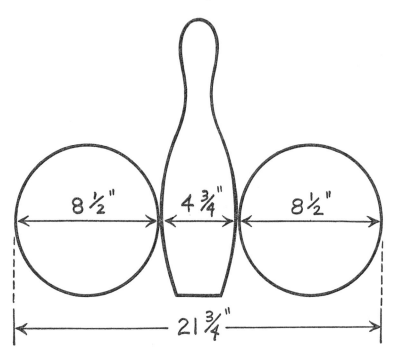

So-called "double wood" spares also deserve special consideration. Double wood is a setup where one pin is found directly in back of another. There are three double wood spares: The 1-5, the 2-8, and the 3-9. When you are confronted with one of these, make your target the "sleeper" pin, the rear pin. Shoot "through" the front pin to get it. Don't try to carom the front pin into the back one. This is a tricky piece of business. Depend on the ball to get them both.

Any variations you attempt should only affect your starting position, not your target, however. Always aim for either the second or third rangefinder from the right side. Adjust this way: If you deliver the ball and it looks to be a normal roll, yet it does not quite come up to pin or pins you're after, move your starting position slightly to the right. On the other hand, if the ball breaks too far to the left, move your starting position more to the left. Your adjustments should always be slight ones, no more than a board or two.

Splits are real trouble for every bowler. (By definition, a split is any combination of pins left standing after the first delivery in which a pin is down immediately ahead or between the combination.) The only way to achieve any degree of success in making spares out of splits is to concentrate. You must focus your attention on hitting your target with perfect accuracy. And, as every bowler knows, sometimes concentration is not enough.

The "baby" splits, the 2-7 and the 3-10 combinations, are the easiest. In each case, try to fit the ball in between the two standing pins. The 4-5, 5-6, and 9-10 are other splits that aren't too great a problem. Aim exactly between the two pins.

The 5-7 and 5-10 split setups are more difficult. With the 5-7, you must hit the 5 on the right-hand side, sliding it into the 7. With the 5-10, slide the 5 pin to the right and into the 10. In each case, adjust your starting target before you shoot. For the 5-7, keep to the right of center; for the 5-10, move to the left of center.

Next in degree of difficulty are the 6-7 and 4-10. For these, follow the same technique as for the 5-7 and 5-10. You have to be a bit more artful, however.

For the 4-7-10 split, aim to hit the 4 pin on the left side, causing it to slide into the 10. The ball should topple the 7 pin. In trying for the 6-7-10, slide the 6 into the 7. The ball must get the 10.

The impossible splits are the ones no bowler tries for, not even the top-flight professional. These are the 7-9, the 4-6, the 8-10, the 4-6-7-10, and the most ghastly one of them all, the 7-10. In each case, play safe; try for only one pin (or two pins, in the case of the 4-6-7-10).

Of course, sometimes a spare is imperative in order to win a game or a match, and in such cases a try at an impossible split is justified. But bear in mind that even the most competent of professionals doesn't make a split like the 8-10 more than once in twenty tries. Never attempt an impossible split unless the pinfall involved is extremely critical.

The spare leaves you must face are often an accurate indication of how you are rolling the ball. For instance, if you leave the 5 pin consistently, it is fairly sound evidence that you are not rolling a good working ball. The ball is not finishing with enough authority. You must get more power into your delivery. Lift as you release.

When your ball leaves either the 7 or 10 pins, it demonstrates that you're not playing the correct angle. When the 10 pin stands after a seemingly solid pocket hit, it can be because your hook isn't breaking in a wide enough arc. When the 7 fails to fall, usually the opposite is true—the ball is hooking too much.

When you leave an 8 pin standing, don't feel badly. There is nothing to be ashamed of, because you did nothing wrong. Toppling the 8 is pretty much a matter of chance. Sometimes it is taken out by the ball, and other times it is carried by the 5 pin. When the 8 pin remains standing on what looks to be a flawless roll, it is because the ball went for the 9 pin instead, while the 5 was simply deflected in the wrong direction.

The 5-8 spare is seldom seen by the accomplished bowler. It's caused by delivering the ball too straight and too slow. What happens is that the ball gets deflected to the right by the 1 and 3 pins. Greater speed, power, and roll are needed.

Splits can happen to anyone, but they are much more common to the average bowler than to the top-flighter. On a strike roll, your ball must power its way through the 1-3 pocket and into the 5 pin. Then the 5 must topple the 8. But a ball that is turned aside by the 1 and 3 pins is likely to leave a split, perhaps the 5-10 or the 8-10. Professionals, with their sharp-breaking hooks, seldom face setups like these.

The cause of the 7-10 or the 4-6-7-10 splits is a lack of accuracy. Each results from an attempted strike ball that hits the headpin dead center.

The importance of spares can't be overestimated. Consider this evidence. It's not at all uncommon for a bowler who averages 140 or so to be just as adept at rolling strikes as a bowler in the 180 class. What often sets them apart is the ability of the latter to make spares. Even the facility to make only single pin spares will enable you to carry an average of 170 or thereabouts.

The only way to improve your spare shooting is to practice. The pinsetting machines at many bowling centers are equipped with a device called an Instruct-o-Mat. When this is in operation, the machine will repeatedly set the one pin or combination of pins the bowler wants. It's the perfect way to practice spare shooting.

Develop a confident attitude toward your spares. I see too many bowlers freeze—grow tense—when confronted with a single pin spare or a tough combination, yet the same bowlers are calm and poised when shooting at a full set. I'm not sure I know why this happens. But shooting for spares is no different than shooting for strikes. All you do is adjust your starting position. Everything else—your stance, approach, and release—is the same.

SUMMING UP

For spares in the center of the lane, use the 5 pin angle.
Stand with your left foot in the center of the approach.

Use the second rangefinder from the right-hand side as your target.

For spares on the left half of the lane, use the 7 pin angle. Stand to the right on the approach. Use the second rangefinder from the right-hand side as your target.

Point your body toward the pins.

Use the same delivery for spares as you do for strikes.

When aiming, "cover" the pin nearest you with the ball, and as many other pins of the setup as you can.

10

THE PERFECT STRIKE

By Ed Lubanski,
ABC Tournament Champion;
World's Invitational Champion

Ed Lubanski turned his back on a promising career in professional baseball to devote his full attention to bowling, and he's never regretted the move. In 1947, Lubanski, a pitcher, won twenty-three games for Wausau in the Wisconsin State League, but his achievements in bowling have been much more spectacular and invariably of major league proportions.

Lubanski first came to national attention while a relative youngster. In 1950, not long after his twenty-first birthday, he teamed with Ed (Sarge) Easter to win the BPAA National Doubles title. He averaged 197 in the twenty-four-game finals.

Lubanski's first important individual championship came in 1958 when he took the World's Invitational crown. The following year he established himself as one of bowling's all-time greats, becoming the second man in history to win three titles in the ABC Tournament. He was a member of the championship team; he won the singles competition with a 764 series, and the all events title with an amazing 2116, a record. He was everyone's choice for Bowler of the Year.

Lubanski was also a member of the team that won the all events championship in the ABC Tournament in 1951. Indeed, the ABC Tournament usually finds Lubanski at his best. He holds a 204 average in twenty years of competition in the event. His average in ABC Masters competition is 201.

In 1962 Lubanski won the Chicago Open, his only victory to date on the professional circuit.

For years a five-step bowler, Lubanski recently changed to a four-step style. He uses a unique grip style; his ball has but two holes (for the thumb and middle finger). "That I'll never change," he says.

His best series to date is 815. His best average is 229, achieved during the 1958–59 season. He boasts eleven ABC-sanctioned 300 games, three of them coming in televised competition.

Ed makes his home in Oak Park, Michigan, a suburb of Detroit. He is married with five children. He is a past president of the Professional Bowlers Association and a member of the Sports Advisory Staff of Sears, Roebuck and Company.

To just about every bowler, any strike is a perfect one, a thing of sheer beauty. But to any person the least bit technically minded about the game, some strikes are more perfect than others. In the not-so-perfect strike, all the pins go down, but it is more a happy accident than anything else.

Of course, it is the flawless strike that you should seek, and to achieve it you must have a strike ball target that is mathematically precise. If you miss such a target by an inch or two, you might get a strike anyway. But if your target is wide, and perhaps a little vague, a miss is going to be costly.

Bowling instruction books tell you that your strike ball target is the 1-3 pin pocket. This is only partly right. Many bowlers take this advice to mean that they should hit the 1 and 3 pins simultaneously. But there is a better way.

What you should try to do is come in high and hit the headpin first. To put it in precise and technical terms, the center of the headpin divides the twentieth board from the right-hand side of the lane (actually the center board of the lane). When you hit the headpin on a strike roll, the center of your ball should be on the seventeenth board, that is, about three inches to the left of the center of the headpin. The ball is hooking at this time, of course.

After the headpin has been toppled, the ball, still hooking, takes out the 3 pin. The center of the ball has almost reached the nineteenth board when the 3 pin is felled.

What happens next follows an unvarying pattern. After

toppling the 1 and the 3, the ball drives to the left and takes out the 5 pin. Here you can see the necessity of rolling a hard-driving ball. Not only must the ball take out the 1 and the 3, it must sail into the 5 with such force that the 5 takes out the 8. Often the 5 pin is called the king pin or the key pin. You must get the 5 with the ball to earn a strike. After toppling the 5, the ball is deflected right and into the 9 pin.

The other pins are felled in this manner:

The 1 pin, after being struck by the ball, is deflected left into the 2 pin; the 2 then carries the 4, and the 4 fells the 7.

The 3 pin takes out the 6, and the 6 topples the 10.

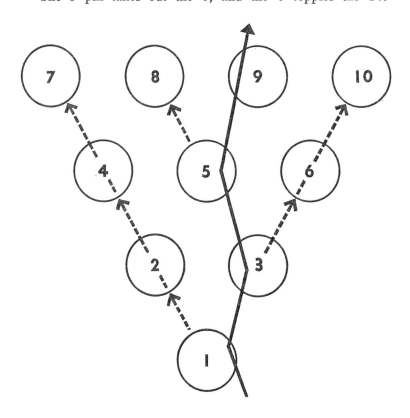

Occasionally the ball will carry the 8 pin in addition to the 1, 3, 5, and 9, but it is virtually impossible for the ball to hit more than five pins, and the more common number is four.

Accuracy is essential in achieving a strike. As every bowler knows, there are times when a tricky spare or a horrendous split will result from what looks to be a faultless hit. Sometimes the 8-10 split results from what is a seemingly perfect roll. When this happens it is because your ball did not hit the headpin squarely enough, though perhaps it was off target by no more than a quarter of an inch. Because it came in too lightly on the 1 pin, the ball was also light on the 5, and this caused the 5 to skitter across the lane in front of the 8, never touching it.

In addition, the ball failed to deflect the 3 pin at the proper angle. As a result, the 6 pin, though felled by the 3, did not take out the 10. All because you missed your target by only a quarter of an inch.

You can also achieve a strike by bringing the ball into the 1-2 pocket, a so-called "Brooklyn" or "Jersey" hit, but the crossover strike depends on pure chance. You will almost always leave pins standing after a 1-2 pocket hit because the ball is hooking away from the 5 pin. If the 5 pin does go down, it is usually because it has been toppled by the 2 pin, not by the ball. A common result of a 1-2 pocket hit is the 3-10 split, not a pretty sight.

Besides knowing what your target is, and hitting it squarely with an effective hook, your ball has to be rolling properly at the time it hits the pins in order to earn your strike. A ball can roll in one of three ways. Each of these is defined in terms of a "track" which appears on the surface of the ball after a game or two. A combination of alley oil and dust, the track reveals your ball to be a spinner, a semi-spinner, or a full roller.

In the spinner, the track is near the bottom of the ball. In the semi-spinner, it is just outside the thumb hole. The track for the full roller encircles the ball between the thumb and finger holes.

THE SPINNER   THE FULL ROLLER   THE SEMI-SPINNER

These variations in roll are caused by the way the ball is released. The semi-spinner, the type of roll for which most bowlers strive, is achieved by having the thumb positioned at eleven o'clock at the moment of release, lifting with the fingers, and turning the wrist in a counterclockwise direction.

Other bowlers prefer the full roller, the ball that rolls like a wheel. This type of ball is achieved by releasing the ball with the thumb in a ten- or eleven-o'clock position, lifting with the fingers, and turning the wrist clockwise. Wrist-turning is a subtle art. It should only be attempted by accomplished bowlers.

If your ball does not pick up a track due to an absence of alley oil, you can learn how it's rolling by affixing a small piece of adhesive tape to the surface, and watching the tape as the ball rolls toward the pins.

Avoid having the ball roll over the thumb hole. This robs it of its power and spoils its accuracy. You can tell this is happening by the thumping sound the ball makes when it rolls, or by examining the track.

A faulty release causes the ball to roll over the thumb

hole. Releasing with more of a counterclockwise turn of the wrist will end the problem.

Of course, there are other factors important in the achievement of strikes. The angle of your hook must be correct (see Chapter 7), and the ball's speed must be right. (It should take the ball between two and 2½ seconds to reach the pins; it travels at about twenty miles per hour.) It's impossible to have absolute control over all of these elements. This is made evident by the fact that there are so few 300 games. But knowing precisely what your target is, and how to roll for it, gives you some advantage and makes those elusive strikes a bit more attainable.

SUMMING UP

To achieve a strike, target on the 1-3 pocket, but aim to hit the headpin first.

Seek to achieve a semi-spinner, a ball that bears a track just outside the thumb. A full roller is also acceptable. In this the track encircles the ball between the thumb hole and finger holes.

11

TIMING AND BALANCE

By Jim Stefanich, WINNER, FIRESTONE TOURNAMENT OF CHAMPIONS, 1966

Sports-minded as a youngster, Jim Stefanich tried golf and baseball before he decided on a career in bowling. The rewards came quickly. In 1962, at twenty, he finished third in the ABC Masters, a stunning achievement. The next year he did even better, rolling a 662 in the team competition of the ABC Tournament's regular division to lead his squad to a first-place finish. In 1964 he won the ABC Tournament's singles crown.

One of Jim's biggest thrills in bowling was being chosen as a member of the U.S. team that competed in the fifth annual World Bowling Tournament, which was held in Mexico City. He placed second. In 1964, competing in the Inter-Americas Tournament in Caracas, Venezuela, an event sponsored by the Fédération Internationale des Quilleurs, Jim teamed with Les Zikes to take the doubles crown. He also was a member of the U.S. squad which captured the six-man team title.

Jim's success as an amateur convinced him to turn professional. His first pro victory didn't come until 1966 when he won the Baltimore Open. He earned $14,510 that year. He also took the ABC Classic doubles crown, teaming with Andy Regoznica.

The year 1967 began in spectacular fashion, with Jim winning the Firestone Tournament of Champions. Jim averaged an incredible 240. First place was worth $25,000. He followed this with victories in the Fort Smith, Arkansas, Open and the Grand Haven, Michigan, Open. When the 1967 summer tour had ended, Jim topped the money winning list with $37,785 in earnings. Little wonder that he is often called the best of bowling's "young Turks."

The next time you visit your neighborhood bowling center, check the follow-through positions of the first ten bowlers you see. Don't be surprised if at least four or five of them are entirely sideways to the foul line as they deliver the ball, and tottering back and forth to keep from going over the foul line. It is a matter of regrettable fact that almost one-half of the people who bowl are guilty of mistakes that disrupt their timing and throw them off balance. Yet these two factors are as essential to successful bowling as a well-fitted ball.

Good timing is not easy to achieve; in fact, it is not even very easy to define. But, in general, timing refers to the total coordination of your footwork and armswing with the purpose of regulating the speed and roll of the ball to produce the most effective results.

Good timing is essential for success in any sport, but this is particularly true in bowling. When Willie Mays's timing is off, he may hit the ball to right-center field instead of to left-center. But when Don Carter is out of time, he can come up with an 8-10 split instead of a strike.

Your timing is letter perfect when the toe of your left foot —your sliding foot—reaches the foul line at the same instant you release the ball on the lane. When this happens you have the potential to deliver an accurate and potent hook. But there is another way to tell when your delivery is properly timed: you can "feel" it. You almost glide to the foul line. Everything is as smooth as silk and the ball is seemingly weightless. After you've pitched, you're in perfect balance. Invariably your scores show that you're in time, too.

Unfortunately, not many bowlers are able to achieve perfect timing. Most are merely adequate in this department. Mistakes in timing are as common in bowling as missed spares. And like missed spares, they happen to everyone—to both the rank amateur and the skilled professional.

Good timing begins with a proper stance. It involves get-

ting your feet in the right position and holding the ball
correctly. If you aren't comfortable and relaxed in the stance,
it is very unlikely your timing will be precise. As you take
your first step, the ball must move into its swing. On the
second step, the ball must pass your right knee, and by the
time the second step is completed, the ball must be well into
the backswing. Your left arm is outstretched to counterbalance the weight of the ball. On your third step, your
speed increases slightly and the ball moves to the top of the

backswing. The bend of your body is greater. The fourth step is often called the timing step. This is where you put it all together. You push off on your right foot, bend your left knee, and slide. At the same time the ball comes forward. As the slide ends, the ball comes to the point of release. This is perfect timing. It involves every phase of your approach and delivery.

The most common cause of timing ills is too much speed. The pros call it "rushing the line." When you are guilty of this, your body arrives at the foul line a second or two before the ball. Such a mistake may merely mean that you won't be able to impart proper lift at the time of release and the ball won't be a good mixer as a result, but when the error is serious, you will have a feeling you are "losing" or dropping the ball. And you may indeed drop it.

The best way to overcome this is to slow the steps of your approach, which is much more easily said than done. One way to learn to slow down is to count off the steps of your approach as you execute each one. Count cadence, in other words. But instead of merely counting "One, two, three, four," count this way: "One thousand one, one thousand two, one thousand three, one thousand." This method of counting should give the proper tempo.

One other way to slow your approach speed is to make your heel touch down on each one of your steps, and then the ball of your feet. If you have ever watched a sprinter run, you may have noticed he strides on the balls of his feet. This is how you attain great speed. The bowler who rushes the line has a tendency to do this, too. But the heel-to-toe approach will slow you down.

Sometimes lengthening the steps in your approach is helpful in making you more deliberate. This method involves making a host of compensating adjustments in the armswing, however, and doing this can lead to complications. I feel that slowing the steps, using either one of the two methods I've outlined, is the easier way.

Women bowlers often make timing errors, but of a different type. Instead of having too fast an approach, they are often too slow. The ball gets to the foul line first. When this happens you can only drop the ball on the lane in innocuous fashion. You should be grateful if it generates enough velocity to reach the pins. I once saw a woman bowl who had an extremely slow approach and a fast armswing, and when she dropped the ball on the lane it rolled so slowly that it eventually stopped. It got stuck on the thumb hole about six feet from the pins.

The worst thing about an approach that is too slow is that it makes it difficult for you to maintain your proper balance. The weight of the ball can become a serious problem. Often it pulls your right shoulder toward the floor. Any time the ball's weight feels burdensome to you, it's a pretty clear indication that you are guilty of a timing error somewhere along the line.

Sometimes you can overcome this problem simply by shortening the steps in your approach. Occasionally this type of timing error is caused by putting the ball into the pushaway before the first step of the delivery is begun. Once a bowler realizes he is doing this, it is not a big problem to get him to start his approach the right way—with his first step and his pushaway beginning together.

Timing problems can also be related to your backswing. The chances are good that if you are rushing the line and speeding the ball you also have a very high backswing. Stand more erect as you take your starting position, but hold the ball at a slightly lower level. Do not bend quite so deeply in the final stages of your approach.

You can also adversely affect your timing if you lunge with the ball on the first or second steps of your delivery or abruptly drop the ball on the lane when you release. You have to slide; you have to release smoothly. From stance to follow-through your actions have to be calm and unruffled. You have to have the feeling that you are gliding to the foul line.

Like timing, balance is related to every phase of your approach and delivery. Good balance begins with the stance. Stand fairly erect. Keep your weight concentrated on your heels, and simply rock forward when you begin your approach. If you're using a four-step delivery, keep your right foot slightly in back of your left to insure that you will step off smoothly. If you're a five-step bowler, there's no necessity to keep one foot ahead. Most people have a natural tendency to step with the left foot on the first stride.

As the ball begins its swing, extend your left arm outward from your body. This counterbalances the weight of the ball. The chances are that you won't have to remember to do this; your left arm will move out naturally.

Balance is also maintained by keeping your steps to a normal length and a moderate speed as you approach. The final step is extremely important. You have to bend your left knee so that you lower your center of gravity. Otherwise you are liable to tilt to one side or the other or go over the foul line. Bending low also helps you to stretch your right leg out in back of you. Remember, it's a knee bend. Bending from the waist can make you top-heavy, and you may even have to move your right foot forward to prevent yourself from toppling. Once you've achieved a proper knee bend and re-leased the ball, stay low as you execute your follow-through.

You can't achieve proper balance if you rush the line. Your steps have to have the proper tempo. Counting cadence —as described above—is the best way to slow your approach.

Another reason bowlers go off balance is drifting, the tendency to angle one's approach instead of following a straight line from the stance to the point of release. Some professional bowlers drift but are able to make up for it one way or another. The average bowler doesn't know how. Suppose you drift to the right. At the last moment you are going to have to twist your body to the left in order to attain a good release and be accurate. But trying to compensate in this fashion is very likely to throw you off balance.

To avoid the inclination to drift, pick out a board in the approach and determine to strike the board with your second and fourth steps—the steps you take with your left foot. By walking a board you'll keep straight.

Your balance can also be upset by an approach that's too short. You arrive at the foul line and find you haven't given yourself enough room to slide. You quickly turn your left foot to the right to prevent it from going over the line. As a result you go off balance. Be certain to give yourself enough room.

Summing Up

Proper timing is achieved when the toe of your sliding foot reaches the foul line simultaneously with your release of the ball. Most errors in timing are caused by too fast an approach. Slow down by counting off your approach steps or by performing them in "heel-to-toe" fashion.

To achieve proper balance, get a solid stance. Keep your weight back on your heels. As you approach, extend your left arm outward. Complete your delivery with a deep knee bend and stretch your right foot out in back of you. Keep low as you execute your follow-through.

12

PRACTICE

By Billy Golembiewski, ABC Masters Champion

Slim and likable Billy Golembiewski—known as Billy "G"—is a familiar figure on the professional tour and one of its most noted performers.

Billy won his first PBA event in Charlotte, North Carolina, in 1963. The next year he won in Columbus, and in 1965 he took the Hialeah Open and the Mobile Open in consecutive weeks.

He owns a splendid record in ABC Tournament competition. He won the ABC Masters title in 1960 and again in 1962, and holds a 206 average in the event. He teamed with Joe Joseph to capture the Classic Doubles crown in 1962, and was a member of the winning team in the ABC event in 1959. His seventeen-year average in ABC Tournament competition is a lofty 201.

He won the Madison Square Garden Tournament in New York City in 1960, 1961 and 1962. He is a member of the Madison Square Garden Hall of Fame.

Billy's best series is an 826, rolled in 1950 when he was twenty-one years old. His best average is 233, attained over the 1958–59 season. He has one ABC-sanctioned 300 game.

Billy was born in Grand Rapids but is now a Detroiter. He is a member of the Bowling Advisory Staff of the Brunswick Corporation.

There is not a soul who disagrees with the contention that the only way to become proficient in bowling is through practice. But not all practice is meaningful practice. There is definitely a right way and a wrong way to conduct a session on the lanes. The wrong way is to be slipshod or haphazard about your bowling. Practice has to be carefully and strategically planned, and you have to be serious-minded about it. That's the only way you can achieve lasting results.

Give some thought to where you practice. Don't pick out a bowling center where the lanes are easy for you; avoid the alley where you bowl regularly. Go to different houses. Learn to cope with a variety of conditions.

If you bowl in one or two leagues and are seeking to boost your average, schedule at least one practice session each week on a regular basis—the same day each week and at about the same time. You are less likely to skip a session when you follow a routine.

Concentrate on just one phase of your game each time you practice. Maybe your release isn't quite right. Maybe you're having backswing problems. Don't worry about pinfall when you practice. This is likely to distract you. Don't even record what pins you fell. Simply check off each frame.

Before I got in the 200 average class, I used to put a great deal of emphasis on spare shooting. This really helped me improve. Spare shooting is perhaps the foremost weakness of the bowler whose average is in the 160–70 range. I would go to a bowling center that had pinboys (there are still a few around) and instruct one to set up the 10 pin fifty times. Or I'd spend a couple of hours shooting at the bucket—the 2-4-5-8. This kind of practice is the only way to become consistent and confident in your spare shooting. You can practice spares at a house that has automatic pinsetting equipment by asking the manager to set the machine for one pin or for a particular combination.

Always be serious about your practice sessions, even when bowling with friends. Don't roll the ball aimlessly—this is a certain way to develop bad habits. Try your best; be competitive. Often the professional bowlers in Detroit get together for an afternoon at the lanes, and we always try to whip one another.

There are remarkably few bowlers who are completely self-taught, which is probably the best argument I know for urging you to have an instructor when you practice. He or she should be someone who has a good knowledge of bowling's fundamentals and is familiar with your style of bowling as well. He should watch you carefully as you bowl. When you approach the foul line and deliver the ball, there are at least one hundred and one things you can do wrong without even knowing it. The average bowler usually commits one of two mistakes. He either rushes the line or he becomes too diligent in his attempt to get the ball to hook. He overturns his wrist. Yet both of these weaknesses are extremely difficult for the individual bowler to detect. It takes an observer to tell when your delivery is awry.

Once, during a streak of poor bowling, one of my teammates came to me and said that I was looping the ball in the backswing, arcing it toward the middle of my back instead of bringing it back on a straight path. As soon as I knew what I was doing wrong, I was able to correct it, but it was the kind of mistake that was virtually impossible for me to spot by myself.

In recent years I've been lucky enough to accumulate five or six different television films that show me bowling. Now when I'm having problems I screen this footage and it usually helps to put me back on the right track. Of course, few bowlers have the opportunity to obtain such an instructional aid, but it's the only other method I've found to be as helpful as having an instructor watch you bowl.

Practice, of course, is also essential when you hit a slump, a prolonged period in which your scoring isn't up to par. Usually this is due to faulty timing. You're rushing; you're at the foul line but the ball isn't. When this happens to me, I cut my speed in half. I practically walk to the foul line. Little by little I increase my speed until I feel I'm back in time. It's a tricky business, however, and it's another instance of where an instructor can be of great help.

One area where practice is of little value is in overcoming the tension that "must" situations create, as when you have to get at least a double in the last frame to win a game or match. Experience is what helps you to master the stresses of pressure. I know that on the pro tour almost every bowler tends to "choke" the first time he competes on television. He may even feel a great deal of tension on his second appearance, but by the ninth or tenth time he doesn't even realize the cameras are there. If tension is your problem, seek out and bowl in the higher-average leagues in your area. Bowl in sweepstakes competition and in tournaments whenever you can. In other words, put yourself in as many tension situations as you can. That's how to conquer pressure.

One additional piece of advice on this subject. I think that many bowlers help to create the problem of tension by being too careful. For instance, the longer you take in getting set to deliver the ball, the greater the likelihood that tension will upset your delivery. "Miss 'em quick" is advice that golf pros give. It applies to bowling, too.

I don't believe a week goes by that someone doesn't ask me how often and how much I practice. My answer always depends on how much I'm bowling in competition. During the weeks that the pro tour is in recess, I might practice as much as thirty or forty games a week. But when I'm on the circuit and bowling thirty to seventy games a week in competition, I don't do very much practicing. There's really no need to, and besides I'd probably just wear myself out. Usually on the Thursday afternoon before a tournament gets under way the lanes are reserved for practice. I spend three or four hours getting the feel of the lanes, establishing a line on each pair. But that is usually the extent of my practice for the week.

Unfortunately, there is very little practice you can do at home. A golfer can practice putt on the living room carpet but a bowler in training is pretty much restricted to the bowling lanes. If you're a beginner in the sport, however, it might be helpful to practice at home with a flatiron, using it as you would your bowling ball. Take a firm grip on the iron and walk through your approach, thrusting it out and down and swinging it back and then forward. Watch out for the furniture!

Summing Up

Schedule your practice sessions on lanes that are unfamiliar to you. That's the way you'll learn. Practice at a regular time each week.

Concentrate in improving only one phase of your approach and delivery in each session. Don't distract yourself by keeping score. Be serious; concentrate.

Most bowlers' faults are difficult for the individual to detect. Try to practice under the supervision of an instructor.

When your scoring ability falls below normal, it is usually because you are rushing the line; your timing is off as a result. Practice walking to the line until you are back in time.

Practice bowling is of little value in helping overcome the stress of tension. You must subject yourself to pressure situations in league play or tournaments to conquer this malady.

13

FOR LEFT-HANDERS

By Roy Lown, WINNER, PBA INVITATIONAL

Late in 1961 at Paramus, New Jersey, Roy Lown won the PBA Invitational, a significant victory in many ways. First prize was fifteen thousand dollars, a record at the time. It was the first PBA event to be nationally televised. But even more important, it was the first PBA tournament ever to be won by a left-hander, and it started a notable trend. Today the pro tour is thickly crowded with southpaws, and while they still may not equal right-handers in quantity, they take down an incredibly high percentage of the prize money. The day of the left-hander has arrived, and Roy Lown was the man who helped usher it in.

Roy was well established as a bowling pro before his victory at Paramus. He won the Kosoff Endurance Classic in 1955, rolling 8014 over the rugged forty-game route. He was a finalist three times in BPAA All Star competition, and twice rolled perfect 300s in the event, a feat no other bowler has accomplished.

He was runner-up on the PBA Open in Kingsport, Tennessee, in 1963, and also was second in the Albany (N.Y.) Open the same year.

He was born in Terre Haute, Indiana, and now makes his home in El Paso, Texas. He owns and operates a bowling-supply store in that city. He has won the El Paso All Events title on five occasions.

Roy has been bowling since 1943. His highest series is a 792. He achieved his highest league average in the 1959–60 season with a 214. During 1966 he averaged 203.6 on the PBA circuit.

The approach and delivery used by left-handed bowlers is simply a mirror image of that used by right-handers, so almost all of the instruction advice concerning the right-hander applies to the leftie but in reverse. The person who uses his left hand more skillfully and in preference to his right, however, soon finds that bowling presents some conditions peculiar to him alone. Fortunately, some of these work to his advantage.

If you have any doubts about that statement all you have to do is take notice of the splendid achievements of left-handers on the pro circuit in recent years. Bill Allen of Orlando, Florida has won a total of nine PBA events. Dave Davis of Phoenix was the sensation of the 1967 summer tour, winning three tournaments and close to forty thousand dollars in prize money. Butch Gearhart of Fort Lauderdale, Florida, won twice on the summer circuit, and with Skee Foremsky, a neighbor of mine from El Paso, was a leading money winner in 1967. Don't overlook John Wilcox, the youngster from Williamsport, Pennsylvania, who won the International Masters Tournament in London in 1966. All are left-handers. According to one set of statistics, left-handers make up approximately 13 per cent of the population, but among professional bowlers the percentage is a great deal higher than that, and more and more are joining the tour every year.

As I've mentioned, conditions are one reason for the success that left-handers have attained. Since most bowling balls are rolled down the right-hand side of the lane, it receives much more wear and tear than the left side. This didn't used to be a serious problem, but today I don't believe that bowling lanes are getting the same careful maintenance they received four or five years ago. Even the ABC has lowered its requirements as to the amount of resurfacing a lane must receive. What this means is that the bowler—the right-hander, at least—can experience a really rough time finding his line. But the left-hander is likely to discover that his side of the lane runs true. No one is crossing his line, and whereas the right-hander has to thread a needle to get a strike, the leftie has a relatively wide pocket.

I don't want to imply that these differences are great. Indeed, they are not, and usually they can only be perceived by the bowler who has had some solid experience in the game. Another factor is important. In order to take advantage of the unflawed conditions on the left-hand side, a bowler has to have genuine talent and deft skill. Certainly not every left-hander who steps up on the approach is able to roll a big game whenever he wants to.

Conditions that the left-hander encounters are likely to be uniform throughout the bowling center—another advantage to the tournament competitor. A right-hander may find that the right side of the lane is fast on one pair and slow on another. It depends on how much play the various pairs get. This means that he has to constantly make adjustments, while the southpaw may find the line that he establishes on one pair works perfectly well on almost every other.

I'm afraid that the first time a left-hander goes bowling he gets the idea that the bowling center is partial to right-handers. You really can't blame him for feeling this way. House balls are drilled out for right hands and not left ones. The hole for the ring finger is always smaller than the hole for the middle finger. This is swell if you're a right-hander, but it can be a problem for lefties. Inevitably the left-hander ends up using a ball in which the fit is less than perfect.

Of course, once a left-hander gets at all serious about bowling, he should purchase a custom-fitted ball. One word of warning, however. A leftie buying a ball should make his purchase in a bowling pro shop, not at a discount house or a department store. I have no special grudge against your local discount store, but I think you will find that the sporting goods department is managed by a man who has to be a specialist in everything from lawn tennis to big-game hunting, and it is farfetched to believe he would know how to measure

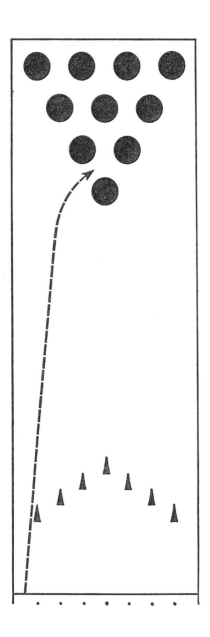

and drill a ball for a left-hander. It takes special knowledge, and that's why the southpaw should seek out a person of experience and reputation.

Bowling shoes are much less of a problem. Those available in the bowling center on a rental basis have a sliding sole on both the right and left shoes. Of course, when a left-hander purchases shoes he has to specify that he wants the sliding sole on his right shoe. In some shops these aren't available as shelf stock, but they are easy for the supplier to obtain on special order.

To achieve a hook, a left-hander must grip the ball with his thumb positioned at about one o'clock. The ball breaks from left to right into the 1-2 pin pocket. Be sure you're behind the ball when you release.

Many people believe that left-handers have more of a natural hook ball delivery than right-handers. I've seen some lefties with really wild hooks, all right, but I've also seen many a southpaw roll a backup ball, a ball that breaks the wrong way, from right to left. I know that in baseball the left-hander has a natural curve, so it is probably true in bowling, too, but no one has ever been able to explain to me just why it is so.

I recommend the four-step delivery, with the bowler stepping off on his left foot. The ball is thrust out on the first step; it goes down and back on the second, rises to the peak of the backswing on the third, and is brought forward for the release as the bowler executes his slide to the foul line. When using a five-step delivery, the bowler begins on his right foot and ends on his right.

While some left-handers use the second rangefinder from the left side of the lane as a target, the trend today is to move to the outside, move one's target to the left. On the pro circuit left-handers often use the third or fourth board from the left side of the lane. Instead of rolling straight down the alley, they point the ball into the pocket. That is, they angle their approach to the pins and roll a ball that breaks only six or seven boards. They do not belly the ball, that is, roll a banana-shaped curve. I would say that about 75 per cent of the pros—both left-handers and right-handers—now shoot mainly from the outside. This method was first brought to prominence by Jim St. John, a right-hander who won the World's Invitational Tournament in 1963 by using this system. He attained a 226 average in the event. No further convincing was necessary.

When I'm bowling on a lane that is faster than normal, I move my stance position to the left slightly. If that doesn't help, I move my targeting spot a board or two to the right. And if both these measures fail to prove effective, I reduce the speed of my ball. I've bowled on lanes that are so fast I've had to resort to all three methods of adjustment at once. When I encounter slow conditions, I move in the opposite direction or increase the ball's speed.

Right-handed and left-handed bowlers both shoot spares from the same starting positions. For spares on the left side of the lane, stand on the right side of the approach. For spares on the right, move left. While right-handers complain about their difficulties with the 10 pin, lefties are bothered by the pin in the opposite corner—the 7. To convert the 7, be certain you're facing the pin as you take your stance. Turn your feet and shoulders toward it. Then as you approach, stride toward it. Roll your normal hook.

I think that left-handers are somewhat discriminated against when it comes to spare shooting. There are dozens of bowling instruction books available, yet I have never seen one that gives advice to southpaws on how to convert tricky leaves. Most bowling center instructors aren't well enough informed to give advice on this subject either. The paragraphs below are an attempt to fill this information gap. They discuss the 5-6, 1-3-6-7, 1-3-9, 2-7, 7-9 and 6-8 setups, somewhat common but difficult spares for the left-hander. The information is of a general nature. Slight modifications might be necessary to fit your game.

The 5-6 results from a ball that fails to finish. Instead of driving through the pocket to topple the 5 pin, the ball was deflected by the 1 and 2 pins. Lack of lift may have been the reason the ball was deficient in power. The way to make the 5-6 is to attempt to fit the ball in between. Take your normal strike stance; move your target four boards to the right.

The 1-3-6-7 is the southpaw's version of the washout. It is likely to happen any time the ball fails to get to the headpin. This is usually a case of the ball lacking in finish, or it may be that the bowler was simply off target. When I'm faced with the 1-3-6-7, I move my stance five boards to the right, and my target four boards to the right. Hopefully the 1 pin will carom into the 7, while the ball will get the 6.

The 1-3-9 is another spare that results from a ball that fails to finish. Instead of coming into the 1-2 pocket, the ball managed only to get the 2, and then it took out the 8. The 5 caromed into the 6, which felled the 10. On the other side of the pindeck, the 2 took out the 4, and the 4 the 7. To convert the 1-3-9, use the same starting position and target as for the 1-3-6-7. In this way the ball will get both the 1 and the 3 and then the 9. You can't count on deflecting the 3 into the 9; the ball must do the work.

The 2-7 is a split but a "makable" one. The result of coming in high on the headpin, the 2-7 is comparable to the 3-10 that right-handed bowlers sometimes face. To convert the 2-7, the trick is to fit the ball in between the two pins. Move to the right corner and aim at the thirteenth or fourteenth boards from the left side. The 2-7 can also be made by hitting the 2 pin on the right side with the idea of deflecting it into the 7, but this is the more difficult way.

The 7-9 split is the sad aftermath of a ball that is accurate enough to hit the 1-2 pocket, but which lacks in spin and roll. Without power or drive, it was deflected into the pit before it could mix the pins. The best procedure here is to go for the 9 pin. For most left-handers the 9 is an easier pin to convert than the 7. Going for both pins is pretty much out of the question.

The 6-8 is usually caused by a ball that finishes with too much hook. Instead of mixing, it sweeps right through the setup. Give the ball a bit more speed. The way to make the 6-8 is to hit the 6 on the right-hand side, deflecting it across the pindeck into the 8. I stand on the tenth board from the right, and shoot for the twelfth board from the right. While the 6-8 is easier to convert than the 7-9 described above, it is not simple by any means.

The starting and targeting positions mentioned above are the ones I use. You may have to adjust them slightly.

Summing Up

The approach and delivery used by a left-handed bowler is simply the reverse of that used by a right-hander. He should use four steps, beginning with a left-foot step and finishing with a right. The ball should be pushed out on step one, down on two, back on three, and released on four.

The left-hand side of the lane is liable to be more slick than the right. Therefore the left-hander must put special emphasis on lifting the ball as he releases in order to get an effective hook.

In general, lane conditions favor the left-hander. Since the left-hand side of the lane receives less play, the ball rolls truer there. Conditions on the various lanes of any one bowling center are likely to be uniform for a leftie.

When buying a custom-fitted ball, the left-hander should be certain to consult a knowledgeable bowling professional.

In aiming, the left-hander usually does best by moving to the outside. His target can be three or four boards from the left side of the lane. Then he must angle his approach and point the ball into the pocket. It should not break more than six or seven boards.

14

FOR WOMEN

By Evelyn Teal, 1961 WIBC ALL EVENTS
CHAMPION

Evelyn Teal holds a number of enviable bowling records and championships, but her most illustrious feat came in winning the 1961 WIBC All Events title. She rolled a 1848—including a 655 in the singles competition—to average 205 over the nine-game route. A resident of Miami, she thus became the first person from the State of Florida to win a national bowling title.

In 1964 she tied for first in the National BPAA All Star competition; however, she lost the three-game rolloff and was placed second.

She is a member of the Professional Woman Bowlers Association and a consistent money-winner on the women's pro circuit. She won the Cavalier Open at New Brunswick, New Jersey, in 1963, averaging 212 over thirty-two games.

She has won virtually every bowling title of significance in her home state. She was Florida State All Events Champion in 1959, and was a member of the Florida State Team Champions in 1960, 1961, and 1962. She was the Miami *Herald*'s Bowler of the Year in 1960 and 1964. In 1967 she captained the Florida State Team Champions.

She is a housewife and a mother. Her daughter Diane was a journalism major at the University of Florida. Golf and water skiing are her other favorite sports. Her highest ABC-sanctioned series is 701; her highest ABC-sanctioned game is 269.

Women are able to excel in bowling because the game puts emphasis on two distinctly feminine traits—grace and rhythm. There is the other side of the coin, however. Women, because they do not have the strength of men, do not have much margin for error when they bowl. Whereas a man can adequately control the ball, even when he makes a mistake in timing, most women can't. Any error a woman commits in the approach inevitably results in a poorly delivered ball. A woman has to develop an approach that is faultless or nearly so. That's why beginning the game correctly, and learning to use those special gifts of rhythm and timing, is so important to the woman bowler.

The woman's first concern has to be in selecting a ball of proper weight and fit. Many do roll a sixteen-pound ball—I do—but most women must use a ball that weighs less. How much less depends on individual factors—her strength and ability to coordinate, and her experience as a bowler.

If she wants, a woman can begin with an eleven- or twelve-pound ball, but as soon as possible—indeed, after just a few games—she should switch to a heavier weight, a ball that weighs 13½ to fifteen pounds. Of course, it stands to reason that the heavier the ball the more pins you will topple, but too much weight can ruin your accuracy and timing. Experiment. Use the heaviest-weight ball you can use without undue effort.

When it comes to purchasing a custom-fitted ball, I don't believe a woman should buy a ball that weighs any less than 13½ pounds. Anything below that weight simply won't carry sufficient pins.

In the bowling clinics I conduct and in private instruction sessions, I always teach women the four-step delivery and the hook ball release. I know this puts me in conflict with some instruction theories, but the four-step, hook ball delivery is the most natural one by far, and I feel it is the easiest to learn. It also happens to be the style that will get you the most pins.

There is a simple test you can perform that will show how completely natural the hook ball release is. Stand erect with your hands at your sides. Now swing your right arm.

Notice how the palm remains facing inward and how the thumb is positioned almost perfectly at ten o'clock. This is what is called the "shake hands" release. This is precisely the way the hook ball is delivered.

Some instructors advise that women bowlers should be taught a straight ball delivery, but to roll a straight ball you have to turn your wrist in a clockwise direction, bringing the thumb to a twelve-o'clock position. This isn't nearly as natural nor as easy to learn as the hook ball delivery.

Another reason I refrain from teaching the straight ball style is because I feel it leads to the development of that horror of horrors, the backup ball, the reverse hook. A woman, in turning her wrist in an effort to get the thumb around to twelve o'clock, is likely to go too far. The thumb swings to two or three o'clcok, and the ball is released with a backup spin as a result. This is much less of a probability when a woman is seeking to achieve a hook ball release.

Of course, in order to roll a hook you have to develop a good amount of speed. Otherwise the ball won't "work." A ball that rolls slowly is very likely to straighten out or fade, and this type of pitch is almost as bad as a backup. To attain the speed necessary to achieve a sharp-breaking hook, a woman has to master a four-step delivery.

There are many women who show a preference for the three-step style. It is fairly common in the East, particularly New England, where duckpins and candlepins, the so-called small ball games, remain in vogue. Three steps are fine when you are bowling with a ball that is about the size of a grapefruit and weighs only three or four pounds. But for a fourteen- or fifteen-pound ball the four-step delivery is essential. It is the only way to assure yourself of an efficient pushaway, and this is the vital part of any woman's delivery.

I encounter many women who have been taught the three-step delivery and have been able to achieve some degree of proficiency with it. I do not try to switch them to four steps. Usually they need to work on moving the ball into the pushaway sooner, but usually any attempt to convert them to a more orthodox style brings on so many problems it is simply not worthwhile.

I recommend that a woman take an upright stance, and avoid the crouch or semi-crouch. When you're erect in the stance, it's easier to execute the pushaway. The feet should be only a few inches apart, and the left foot should be slightly ahead of the right. The weight should be well back on the heels. The weight of the ball should be supported by the left hand.

One common fault that women have is allowing the right wrist to "break" as the fingers are placed in the finger holes. This, too, encourages a backup ball delivery. The ball should be positioned at release. This means the wrist must be perfectly straight.

Once the stance is set, the pushaway is executed. No part of the delivery is more important to the woman bowler. Since women lack in arm and wrist strength, they cannot power the ball through the armswing as some men are able to do. Women have to rely on the ball's momentum, and the only way to achieve this momentum is to thrust the ball out to the full length of the right arm as the very first step of the approach is taken. This—in essence—is the pushaway. The average woman cannot bowl well without it.

In the years that I have been teaching bowling, I have had countless women tell me they can't enjoy the game because "the ball is too heavy." Women who have this complaint usually start their delivery by dropping the ball straight down to the side. Do this and the ball will surely feel twice as heavy as it actually is. The pushaway overcomes this problem. When the ball is thrust out in front of you and gets swinging, the weight of the ball is hardly noticeable.

After a full pushaway on the first step, the ball swings back on the second step. The right hand maintains the same

position that it had in the stance—that is, the wrist is straight and the thumb set for a hook ball release. The ball must be in its pendulum swing at this stage. Here many women commit a serious error. Instead of getting the ball to swing, they carry it in front of them, in somewhat the same way a person might carry a bundle of groceries home from the supermarket. You cannot delay the downswing. When you do, the entire delivery goes awry.

On the third step it is a good idea to accelerate a bit. In this way you build your momentum, and this will give you a more effective release. Your left arm should be fully outstretched. This helps you to maintain your balance.

Let the ball swing back to the peak of the backswing. It must swing almost to the level of your shoulders. If it doesn't go that high, you won't be able to achieve any real speed.

Your arm must be perfectly straight all the way from your shoulder to the back of your hand. This enables you to get a free-swinging ball. If you notice any strain in your elbow as the ball swings, it's an indication your arm is not perfectly straight.

Many women, once they become somewhat proficient in the approach, develop a backswing that is much too high. The ball looks like it is going to rocket into the ceiling. Marion Ladewig, surely the greatest woman bowler of recent times, if not of all time, once had a backswing that saw the ball climb to a position almost straight over her head. To cure this her instructor recommended that she shorten her steps and try more of a normal walking pace. The advice worked, and not long after, Marion won the first of a long, long string of national titles. If your backswing is too high, try shortening and slowing your steps.

The fourth step is actually a long, smooth slide. As you slide, bring the ball forward. Release. Follow through.

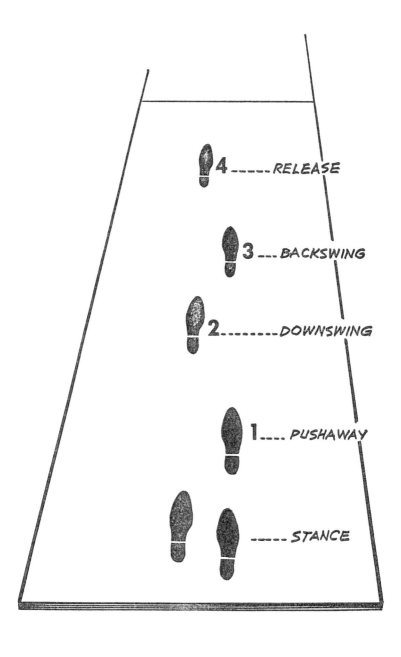

4 _ _ _ _ _ RELEASE

3 _ _ _ BACKSWING

2 _ _ _ _ _ _ _ _ DOWNSWING

1 _ _ _ _ PUSHAWAY

_ _ _ _ _ STANCE

Failing to bend low to the lane is the most grievous error women make at this stage. You must bend low to get a smooth release. I think the problem here has to do with woman's vanity. They feel they might look awkward or un-feminine or both. But you cannot be timid or tense when you bowl. You must look and act like you mean business. And at the final stage of the delivery, this means you must bend your left knee deeply when making your slide. Never bend just from the waist.

I instruct women to spot bowl, not to target on the pins. At first many of them don't believe that aiming for a range-finder is the better way, but their confidence builds quickly after three or four successful rolls. When a woman has trouble hitting her target, I walk out on the lane and put my toe on the spot. Then I say, "Just roll the ball over my foot." It's astonishing how much and how quickly their ability to concentrate improves. Of course, once they roll, I take away my foot. Women should spot bowl for both strikes and spares, not just for strikes.

No woman can bowl wearing a tight sheath or a blouse with a sleeve that restricts the armswing—yet I see many women try to. At one time there might have been an excuse for this. Women bowlers of a decade or so ago were advised to wear "a loose-fitting blouse and a full skirt," certainly not an attire for the fashion-minded. Today it's very different. A woman can select smart bowling outfits that would be the pride of a Paris model. Poor boy sweaters, hipster shirts, and trim, tailored culottes are among the styles available. Even the colors—deep eggplant, avocado, and pimento—suggest bowling's high-fashion bent. "Sew and bowl" fashions are also on the market, with patterns featured in the noted Butterick line. That's not all. In recent years bowling bags and shoes for women have turned chic and fashionable. Many bowling centers now feature a wide array of color-matched shoe and bag sets.

Once a woman has gained some facility with the bowling ball, she should consider joining a league. I began bowling in leagues when I was a teen-ager, and I can assure you that there is no better way to take advantage of the fun and excitement bowling has to offer. League bowling is not expensive; it seldom costs more than two dollars a week, including the cost of bowling three games. And women's leagues are scheduled on an almost around-the-clock basis —morning, afternoon, and evening. Don't feel that bowling leagues are only for the beginner. Nothing could be farther from the truth. Indeed, most bowling centers offer at least one league for novice women. Ask your local proprietor about the types of leagues he has available. Incidentally, most bowling centers have nurseries or baby-sitting facilities of some type where a mother can leave her youngster.

When you join a league (and pay a $1.75 fee) you automatically become a member of the Woman's International Bowling Congress, the organization that oversees women's bowling in this country. Besides setting rules and regulations for women's leagues, the WIBC conducts an enormous awards program that gives recognition to women who roll high scores or perform other outstanding bowling feats. For instance, if you convert the tricky 4-6-7-10 split, you win a woven emblem for the sleeve of your bowling blouse. The WIBC was organized in 1916, and today boasts a membership of close to three million. Who says that bowling is a man's sport? For more information concerning the organization, write WIBC headquarters, 1225 Dublin Road, Columbus, Ohio 43212.

I'm constantly running into women who have become disenchanted with bowling. They have tried the sport and found the weight of the bowling ball to be a discouraging problem. Or they are self-conscious. When they bowl, they feel they are a frenzy of flailing arms and wobbly legs, and that every single person in the bowling center is staring at them. This is unfortunate, because bowling has so much to offer the average woman. It's doubly regrettable because most of the difficulties women have with the game can be easily overcome. If the woman novice would simply take the time to get some solid instruction, getting a good grounding in the use of the four-step delivery and the execution of the pushaway, her problems with the game would be insignificant. Bowling is mainly a case of knowing the fundamentals and executing them with the proper rhythm and timing. It's as simple as that.

Summing Up

A woman should select a bowling ball light enough so it can be easily controlled, but heavy enough to carry pins. For most women this means a ball between 13½ and fifteen pounds.

Women should seek to develop a hook ball release, holding the ball with a "shake hands" grip. The four-step delivery is recommended.

The pushaway is the key phase in any woman's delivery. On the first step she must thrust the ball out to the full length of her right arm. By getting the ball into its proper swing, she assures she will roll the ball with sufficient speed.

Bending the left knee on the final step—the slide—is a must. It makes for a smooth release.

Women should spot bowl on both strikes and spares.

In general, a woman requires a good grounding in the fundamentals of bowling, and the knowledge of how to make use of two womanly attributes, rhythm and timing.

15

FOR JUNIORS

By Mike Durbin, WINNER, YOUNGSTOWN OPEN

The year 1967 was twenty-six-year-old Mike Durbin's first on the pro tour, and the pace he set was the envy of many a veteran. He did so well that at year's end Mike was named the PBA's Rookie-of-the-Year and voted Southern California Bowler of the Year.

Mike won the Tampa Bay Open and the Youngstown Open, and was runner-up in the New Orleans Open. Through a good part of 1967, he was the tour average leader, setting a 214-plus pace.

Mike was brought up in Burbank, California, and now makes his home in Costa Mesa. In 1966 he won the Costa Mesa tournament in Pacific Coast professional competition.

Thanks to the tremendous number of junior bowling instruction programs available today, there's no reason a youngster can't become thoroughly grounded in bowling's fundamentals. The American Junior Bowling Congress operates an impressive number of clinic programs, and virtually every community has its corps of highly trained junior instructors.

I can't stress too much the importance of good instruction for the beginning bowler. Any youngster seeking to develop a bowling style completely on his own is asking for trouble.

Almost every center has at least one staff member who specializes in teaching the game. Choose one that's properly qualified. Many instructors have taken special courses in junior instruction given by the American Junior Bowling Congress or similar organizations. These instructors can be identified by special arm patches they wear or certificates displayed at the bowling center where they are employed.

It is relatively unimportant whether the instructor is a top-notch bowler. The qualities that make a skillful instructor are not necessarily those that enable one to roll high scores. The instructor only has to have the knowledge of how to roll strikes, not the physical prowess to do it himself. Some people can do both, of course, but it doesn't happen very often.

Besides having a complete understanding of how the game is played, an instructor must possess a good amount of patience. He has to be willing to explain the basics of the sport time and again. A fledgling bowler should listen to only one instructor. Someone once said that bowling is a game with as many instructors as participants. Indeed this is true. Everyone is willing to help. But taking advice from too many people is just as harmful as taking no advice at all.

I was a late starter; I didn't begin bowling until I was fifteen. About once a week, my dad used to take me to a neighborhood bowling center in Burbank, California, where I was brought up. It's difficult to say at what age a youngster can begin to bowl. Some have enough strength and coordination to shoot well at seven or eight, others not until they're ten or eleven.

No youngster should be introduced to the game until he or she is able to approach the foul line and deliver the ball in the conventional way. I've seen youngsters carry the ball to the foul line with two hands, as if they were carrying a bushel basket, and thud it onto the lane. A youngster caught up in this kind of an experience quickly sours on the game. It's hard on the lane, too.

I think a youngster's attitude toward the game is extremely important. My dad used to tell me over and over, "Remember, it's only a game. Take your time; have fun!"

It seems to me that most youngsters are too much concerned with how many pins they can knock down. Scores are all-important to them. Instead, the boy or girl beginner should concentrate on timing—on the coordination of footwork and arm action.

Most youngsters race to the foul line in their effort to score. They figure the faster their steps, the faster the ball will roll. And ball speed, they believe, is what topples pins. Of course, this theory is completely wrong. Timing and accuracy are what are important. I was told to pause before I took my first step, to sight my target, and to make up my mind I was going to roll the ball over it. This advice slowed me down.

The importance of bowling courtesy must be stressed to many youngsters. Too often they aren't serious enough about the game. By cheering or jeering one another, they distract bowlers on adjacent lanes. The gyrations they perform at the foul line annoy other bowlers. Often they are careless with food or drink, spilling it on the floor. One reason that youngsters don't conduct themselves with restraint is because they fail to realize that bowling is a game that requires intense concentration. They have to be made to appreciate the fact that good manners will make the game more enjoyable for themselves, as well as for others.

A youngster beginning the game should have the bowling-center equipment explained to him, too. He should be taught the difference between house balls, those owned by the bowling center, and those owned by individual bowlers. It prevents mixups. He should be taught the proper way to pick up a ball, grasping it with both hands on the sides facing away from adjacent balls on the return rack. This method assures his fingers won't be struck by the balls being returned from the pit area. He should be told the basics of the operation of the automatic pinsetting equipment. Quite often I see youngsters "double ball" the machine. Using someone else's ball, they try for a spare before the machine has reset the

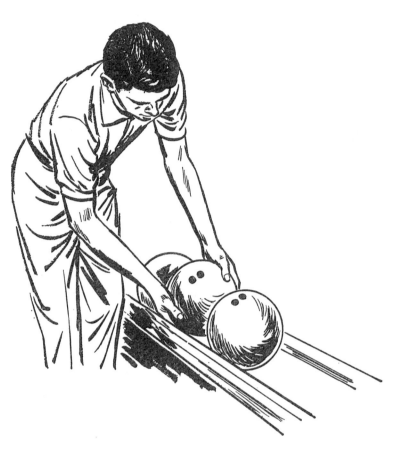

pins. This can damage the machine. They should be instructed in how to cycle the machine to get a full set of pins. The use of the "trouble button" should be demonstrated.

Getting a ball of the right weight for a youngster is not difficult. All bowling centers have junior-weight balls available. The lightest of these is nine pounds, although eight- and even six-pound balls have recently been put on the market. The heaviest junior balls weigh twelve pounds. The weight of each ball bears a very close relationship to the size and location of the thumb hole and finger holes. For instance, a ball in which the thumb hole is relatively large and quite far apart from the finger holes is a ball for a big person. It will be quite heavy. But when a youngster picks out a ball with a satisfactory finger fit, the weight is very likely to be suitable, too.

The ball should fit in the same way an adult ball does. The fit of the thumb should be a little bit on the loose side. There should be only slight friction between the thumb and the sides of the thumb hole. The fit of the fingers should be tighter.

To determine if the span of the ball is the right size, the young bowler should insert his thumb, and then insert his fingers to the second knuckle. He should then try to slide a pencil between his palm and the ball. If the pencil just slips in between, the ball fits properly.

Like every youngster, I first used a house ball, and it had a conventional grip. After I had been bowling for a year or so, I bought a custom-fitted ball. It's debatable whether a youngster should own his own ball. When an adult buys a ball, he figures on prorating its cost over several seasons. This policy doesn't apply when puchasing a junior ball, however. Usually the youngster is developing so fast that his fingers and hand will be too big for the ball after just one season.

When a youngster outgrows a ball all is not lost, however. Often the ball can be refitted, not a difficult matter. The pro in a bowling-supply shop merely plugs and redrills the thumb hole, positioning it so the span is wider. Then the finger holes are enlarged. Such a refitting operation costs about five dollars.

Very few youngsters are skilled enough to be able to use the fingertip grip or the semi-fingertip. These styles require more than the average amount of arm and finger strength, plus the experience gained in bowling in league play at least two or three times a week.

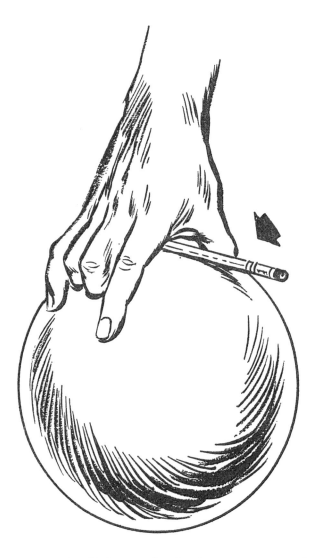

Youngsters should be taught the four-step approach, the very same one that adults use. When I was learning the four-step, I had an instructor who told me, "Get the ball out on one, down on two, and back on three. On four slide and release." I got so I would count—slowly—"one, two, three, four" as I went to the foul line, and perform the appropriate action on each step.

By "out on one" the instructor meant me to thrust the ball away from my body on the first step, to execute the pushaway; "down on two" directed me to get the ball into the downswing, and "back on three," to arc the ball into the backswing. On fourth or final step, the slide, I was to bring the ball forward and release it. Even today, when I'm having problems with my timing, I revert to the simple basics of the approach, and as I stride to the foul line I count a slow cadence to get the tempo of my delivery back on the beam.

Fortunately, I was taught to spot bowl right at the beginning. Most youngsters are pin bowlers because it's the natural way to bowl, and nobody bothers to try to change them. But I believe a youngster will have much greater success if he learns to target at a spot on the lane near him than if he aims directly at the pins. Don't wait to instruct a youngster in the spot system. The longer the young boy or girl keeps to the pin technique, the more difficult it is to switch.

The question that young bowlers ask me the most is, "How do I learn to roll a hook ball?" I tell them to simply turn their thumb to the left as they release. If a youngster has had some experience in the sport, I explain in greater detail. I tell him to release with the thumb at ten or eleven o'clock, keeping his fingers beneath the ball as he comes through.

Joining the American Junior Bowling Congress is a good way for a youngster to learn most of what there is to know about organized bowling. The AJBC offers a comprehensive program of league and tournament bowling. There are more than fifteen hundred communities where AJBC services are available. Inquire at your local bowling center as to what activities the AJBC sponsors in your locality.

Almost every bowling center has at least one AJBC league. Competition is divided into three age groups: Bantams, twelve and under; Juniors, thirteen to fifteen; and Seniors, sixteen to eighteen. It costs only twenty-five cents to join an AJBC league, and each young bowler receives a membership card and a chance to share in the organization's vast awards program. Every year the AJBC distributes about three hundred thousand award certificates, medals, emblems, and trophies for outstanding team and individual achievement. A youngster who joins the AJBC and shares in the outpouring of prizes doesn't have to worry about his athletic eligibility, because the AJBC programs have been sanctioned by the National Federation of High School Athletic Associations. For more information about the junior congress, write AJBC, 1572 East Capitol Drive, Milwaukee, Wisconsin, 53211.

Today bowling is more popular with youngsters than ever before. Membership in the AJBC is climbing to record levels. Not only are more boys and girls bowling than ever, but they're bowling better. In 1967 they accomplished some stunning feats. Mert Carroll, a seventeen-year-old from Hialeah, Florida, rolled the highest series ever bowled by a girl in sanctioned AJBC competition, a 724, on games of 268, 188, and 268.

Jimmy Nelson, a fifteen-year-old Fort Irwin, California youngster and a bowler for only eighteen months, turned in an astonishing 812 series during the year, an all-time AJBC record. He had games of 266, 247, and 299.

Gary Aikin, an AJBC member from Supulveda, California rolled a 300 game. Juniors have rolled 300s before, but never had the feat been performed at so tender an age. Gary was fourteen.

These achievements are convincing proof of the great value of junior bowling instruction when combined with the excitement and enthusiasm of league competition.

SUMMING UP

Junior bowlers should strive for timing and accuracy. Achieving high scores should be of secondary importance.

Junior bowlers should use a ball with a conventional grip, be taught to spot bowl, and deliver a hook ball.

Juniors should learn the four-step delivery, getting the ball "Out on one, down on two, and back on three. On four, slide and release."

16

KEEPING SCORE

By *Johnny Meyer,* WINNER, HOUSTON OPEN

Johnny Meyer had to borrow airplane fare to get to Houston for his first PBA tournament. He became quickly solvent, however, for the tall left-hander won first place and $4000 in prize money. His earnings for the year totaled $11,465.

In 1965, a year highlighted by his victory in the Brockton, Massachusetts, Open, Johnny compiled $11,785 in money winnings.

Johnny's hometown is Lake Ronkonkoma, New York. He has rolled one ABC-sanctioned 300 game.

Anyone who is the least bit serious about bowling knows the first principles of keeping score, e.g., a game consists of ten frames, a strike is worth ten pins plus the total pinfall on the next two deliveries, etc. But knowing only the fundamentals of scoring is not sufficient. If you want to be able to achieve your highest average, you should record the results of each of your games in the most minute detail.

In other words, your score sheet should not only report the amount of your score, it should also give you a detailed analysis of how that amount was achieved. It should tell you how you performed. This information has real value. By checking over a carefully detailed score sheet at the end of an evening's play, you can sometimes detect one or more weaknesses in your game. Perhaps you are fouling in the late frames or in pressure situations. Perhaps multiple pin spare shots are one of your shortcomings. Or it may be that you are being victimized by splits more than is normal. This is only a sample of the intelligence you can derive from a score sheet. Your own memory can be faulty, but the score sheet is infallible when it comes to recalling what happened and how.

Keeping a very detailed account of your game is more than personally valuable. It also reduces scoring errors and facilitates any auditing of the score which might be necessary. In fact, in league and tournament play, the rules of the American Bowling Congress make mandatory that both first and second ball counts be recorded (when a strike or spare is not registered in the frame). Says the ABC, "The number of pins knocked down after the first delivery, before the player bowls at the remaining pins, should be marked in the upper right corner of the frame. The count in every frame where an error is committed shall be recorded immediately following the player's second delivery."

First, some fundamentals. A game of bowling consists of ten frames. You are "up" ten times. In each frame, you deliver the ball twice, unless you knock down all the pins with your first ball. This is a strike.

An exception to this rule occurs in the tenth frame. If you roll a strike or spare in the tenth frame, you are entitled to an extra roll—a third ball.

The ten frames of the game are represented on the score sheet by a string of boxes numbered from one to ten. In the upper right-hand corner of the box are two smaller boxes. Use both of these in keeping score, not just one of them. The number of pins toppled with the first delivery in a frame should be recorded in the first of the small boxes. The pinfall achieved on the second delivery should be recorded in the second small box.

It must be said that some bowling centers do not provide "double box" score sheets, only "single box" ones. In such cases, simply record the number of pins knocked down on the first delivery just to the left of the box.

STRIKE   SPARE   ERROR   SPLIT   FOUL

Scorekeeping is done with the help of symbols, a kind of bowling shorthand. There are five symbols to know:

A *strike* is indicated by a cross or an "x." The next ball delivered begins the new frame. When you bowl a strike, you are credited with a count of ten, plus whatever pinfall you achieve on your next two rolls of the ball.

A *spare* is recorded on the score sheet with a diagonal line (/). If you knock down all the pins with your two deliveries in a frame, it is a spare. You are credited with a count of ten, plus whatever pinfall you achieve on your next delivery.

An *error* (also called a miss or a blow) is marked with a short horizontal line, a dash (-). This occurs whenever you fail to topple all the pins with your two deliveries. You receive credit only for those pins you've knocked down. There are no bonus pins, in other words.

A *split* is indicated by a circle (0). By dictionary definition, a split is any combination of pins left standing after the first delivery, with a pin down immediately ahead or between the combination. More succinctly, a split is an arrangement of pins, so separated as to make a spare almost impossible. Should you fail to convert the split, that is, should you leave one or more pins standing after your second roll, it is technically not an error. But the scoring is the same as if it were an error: you receive credit only for those pins toppled.

A *foul* is indicated on the score sheet by the letter "F." You are charged with a foul any time you cross or even "encroach upon" the foul line, or come in contact with the lane or any piece of equipment on the lane side of the foul line. The penalty is severe. No pins toppled on that delivery are to be counted.

To give you a better understanding of how to keep carefully detailed score, a sample game is reported below frame by frame.

FRAME 1—With your first roll, you topple all the pins—a strike. You receive credit for 10 pins, plus a bonus of the total number of pins toppled on the next two balls. No score can be recorded until you complete these two deliveries.

①	②
☒	☒
30	56

FRAME 2—A second strike. Another bonus delivery must be completed before your score for the first frame can be recorded. And two bonus balls must be rolled before your score for the second frame can be set down.

①	②	③
☒	☒	☒
30	56	75

FRAME 3—A third strike. Now you can complete your first-frame score. You received 10 pins for your original strike, plus 10 pins for each of the two bonus balls—a total of 30 pins in the first frame. Your score in the second and third frames cannot be recorded yet.

①	②	③	④
⊠	⊠	⊠	6
30	56		

FRAME 4—You topple 6 pins with your first ball. A "6" goes in the first of the small boxes inside the fourth-frame box. Now you can record your score for the second frame. It is 26 pins—a count of 10 pins for the strike, plus a count of 10 pins achieved with the first bonus ball and plus a count of 6 pins achieved with the second bonus delivery. This gives you a total of 56 when added to your first-frame count.

①	②	③	④
⊠	⊠	⊠	6 3
30	56	75	84

With your second ball in the fourth frame, you topple 3 pins. This gives you a total of 9 pins for the frame. Now you can record both your third- and fourth-frame totals.

①	②	③	④	⑤
⊠	⊠	⊠	6 3	@ /
30	56	75	84	94

FRAME 5—You knock down 8 pins with your first ball, but a split remains. With your second delivery, you topple the standing pins and score a spare. Your score cannot be recorded until after your next roll.

①	②	③	④	⑤	⑥
⊠	⊠	⊠	6 3	@ /	F 8
30	56	75	84	94	102

FRAME 6—On your first ball, you foul. Any pins knocked down do not count. The foul also washes out the bonus pins you would have received for your spare in the fifth

frame. Now you can record your score in Frame 5; it is 10 pins. On your second roll in Frame 6, you topple 8 pins, and that is your total for the frame.

①	②	③	④	⑤	⑥	⑦
⊠	⊠	⊠	6 3	@ /	F 8	8 /
30	56	75	84	94	102	

FRAME 7—After toppling 8 pins with your first ball, you spare.

①	②	③	④	⑤	⑥	⑦	⑧
⊠	⊠	⊠	6 3	@ /	F 8	8 /	⊠
30	56	75	84	94	102	122	

FRAME 8—A strike. Now you are able to record your score for the seventh frame.

①	②	③	④	⑤	⑥	⑦	⑧	⑨
⊠	⊠	⊠	6 3	@ /	F 8	8 /	⊠	9 -
30	56	75	84	94	102	122	141	150

FRAME 9—You topple 9 pins with your first ball, but with your second roll you fail to topple the one remaining pin. An error is recorded. Now you can complete your score through the ninth frame.

①	②	③	④	⑤	⑥	⑦	⑧	⑨	⑩	TOTAL
⊠	⊠	⊠	6 3	@ /	F 8	8 /	⊠	9 -	X X 9	
30	56	75	84	94	102	122	141	150	179	179

FRAME 10—Your first roll of the frame is a strike. You have two bonus deliveries coming. On the first one, you strike again. On the second, you topple 9 pins. Your score for the frame is 29. Your score for the game is 179.

In league competition, scorekeeping often has one additional feature. A running total of marks—strikes and spares —is kept. This enables the competing bowlers to keep a somewhat accurate tally of how a match stands. Each mark, each strike or spare, that is, is worth approximately 10 pins. Thus should Team A (with five members) be leading Team B, 43 marks to 40, Team A's advantage would be about 30 pins.

In this system, a double (two consecutive strikes) counts 2 marks in the frame in which it occurs. And when bowler scores 5 pins or less after a spare or on the first delivery after a strike, one mark is deducted from the team's total.

Summing Up

A game consists of ten frames. Each box on the score sheet represents one frame.

You bowl two balls in each frame, unless your first delivery is a strike; that is, unless you topple all the pins with your first ball. A spare is felling all the pins with two balls.

If you get a strike, your score for that frame is 10, plus the total pinfall you achieve on your next two deliveries.

If you get a spare, your score for that frame is 10, plus the total pinfall you achieve on your next delivery.

If you fail to topple all 10 pins in a frame, you merely record the number you did knock over. That is your score for that frame.

The score of the game is carried over from frame to frame.

17

COURTESY AND ETIQUETTE

By Glenn Allison, ABC TOURNAMENT CHAMPION

Glenn Allison has ranked as one of the nation's better bowlers for almost a decade, and his superior knowledge of the game has earned him the esteem of his fellow professionals. He's known as "a bowler's bowler."

Glenn's first victory in PBA competition came in 1962 when he won the Memphis Open. Since then his PBA tournament victories have included: Salt Lake City Open (1962), Oklahoma City Open (1963); Tucson Open (1964), and the Oxnard, California, Open (1964). He ranks eleventh on the all-time PBA money-winning list.

Glenn also owns an outstanding record in ABC Tournament competition. In 1958, 1964, and 1966 he was a member of the ABC Classic team champions. In 1962 he shared the Classic doubles title with Dick Hoover.

Glenn's game lacked its usual sharpness during part of 1966, but the following year he returned to championship form, winning back-to-back titles on the Pacific Coast professional bowling circuit.

Glenn's best series is a 793; he has one ABC-sanctioned 300 game to his credit.

Every sport has its rules of good conduct, and bowling is no exception. They help to make the game more enjoyable and safer.

About everyone agrees that the most important rule of bowling's courtesy code is the right-of-way rule. It dictates that the bowler on the lane to your right has the privilege of bowling first when you and he are getting set to bowl at the same time. You must always defer to the person on your right unless he signals you—with a nod of his head— that you may bowl first.

Bowlers, for the most part, are careful to observe the right-of-way rule. They're not so careful in obeying the rule that states that you should stay off the approach while a bowler on an adjacent lane is getting set to bowl. Many bowlers merely keep to the rear of the approach; they do not move completely off it. This can be very distracting to the bowler who is taking aim.

After you've delivered the ball, keep your "body English" to a minimum. Never let your gyrations become so enthusiastic that you cross onto an adjacent approach. It's not only distracting; it can be dangerous.

Always be punctual. You spoil the fun of others when you arrive late.

Never "double ball" the automatic pinspotter. That is, do not use someone else's ball to try for your spare before the sweep bar rises. Youngsters are sometimes guilty of this. Bowl at the pace set by the machine.

Never use powder or resin to condition the approach. If conditions aren't to your liking, speak to the manager of the lanes.

Courtesy also refers to the practice of encouraging the players with whom you are bowling. Perhaps you've noticed that practice is quite prevalent on the pro tour, even when the stakes are very high. Bowlers using the same pair of lanes will cheer on one another. They are not boisterous, of course, but quiet phrases like "Good shot," or "Nice game," are fairly common.

On the other hand, I've never heard one pro bowler criticize another. I've never heard a word of ridicule.

Professional bowlers are always very willing to help one another improve. Hank Lauman, Joe Kristof, Steve Nagy, and Billy Welu gave me advice that increased my know-how. I try to help upcoming bowlers whenever I can. But I never volunteer advice. I don't believe any bowler should. Wait until you're asked.

These rules of courtesy are universally recognized. Following them helps to make the game more enjoyable and safer.

18

RULES AND REGULATIONS

(The rules and regulations presented in this section are a condensed version of the General Playing Rules of the American Bowling Congress.)

Equipment Specifications

A regulation bowling lane, including the flat gutters, kickbacks and approach, shall be constructed of wood. The edge of the pindeck, tail plank, kickbacks, flat gutters, and gutter moldings may be reinforced with fiber or other synthetic material, however.

The over-all length of a regulation bowling lane shall be 62 feet, $10\frac{3}{16}$ inches from the foul line to the pit, with a one-half-inch tolerance in length permitted. The lane shall be $41\frac{1}{2}$ inches in width with a one-half-inch tolerance permitted. A maximum tolerance of 40/1000 inch is permitted in the levelness of the lane.

The approach shall be not less than 15 feet in length. A tolerance of one-quarter inch is permitted in the levelness of the approach.

The foul line shall be not less than three-eighths nor more than one inch in width. It must be clearly and distinctly marked upon or embedded in the lane. It shall extend from the lane to and upon any walls or posts adjoining or within reach of the bowler.

The pins spots upon which the pins are to be spotted shall be clearly and distinctly marked or embedded in the lane. Each shall be 2¼ inches in diameter. It shall be twelve inches from the center of one spot to the center of each adjacent spot.

Bowling pins shall be made of sound, hard maple. Each shall be constructed from one piece or be of laminated construction with two or more pieces being used. The standard wood pin and the plastic-coated pin must weigh not less than 3 lbs., 2 ozs. nor more than 3 lbs., 10 ozs. The synthetic pin must weigh not less than 3 lbs., 4 ozs., nor more than 3 lbs., 6 ozs. Pins must not vary more than four ounces in each set, and must be uniform in construction, appearance, finish, labeling, and neck marking. The height of each pin shall be 15 inches, with a tolerance of 1/32 inch permitted.

A regulation bowling ball shall be constructed of a nonmetallic composition material. It shall have a circumference of not more than 27 inches, and shall weigh not more than 16 pounds. Tampering with a bowling ball to increase its weight or to cause it to become off balance is prohibited. Plugs may be inserted for the purpose of redrilling the ball, and designs may be embedded in the ball to serve as guides or for identification purposes, but these must be made flush with the outer surface of the ball and must be composed of material similar in nature to the material of which the ball is composed. No foreign material may be placed on the outer surface of the ball. Any ball that does not conform with any of these provisions may not be used in leagues or tournaments sanctioned by the American Bowling Congress.

Scoring the Game

The game of American Tenpins shall consist of ten frames. Each player shall bowl two balls in each of the first nine frames, except when he scores a strike. A player who scores a strike or a spare in the tenth frame shall deliver three balls.

A ball is legally delivered when it leaves the bowler's possession and crosses the foul line into playing territory.

A strike is recorded when a player completes a legal delivery and fells the pins on the first roll of a frame.

A spare is scored when the bowler topples all the pins with the two balls of a frame.

An error is recorded when the bowler fails to topple all the pins with his two deliveries of a frame, provided the pins left standing do not constitute a split.

A split is a setup of pins wherein:

—at least one pin is down between two or more of the pins that remain standing, as in the 7-9 or 3-10 setups.
—at least one pin is down immediately ahead of two or more pins that remain standing, as in the 5-6 setup.

Illegal Pinfall

When any of the following incidents occur, the ball is to be registered as a ball rolled, but the pins knocked down do not count:

—The bowler fouls.
—The ball rebounds from the rear cushion.
—The ball leaves the lane before reaching the pins.
—The pinspotter topples a pin.
—Pins which are bowled off the lane but rebound to a standing position on the lane must be counted as pins standing.

Dead Ball

Any pinfall achieved by a ball that has been declared dead does not count. After the pins have been respotted (and the cause for declaring the ball dead has been removed) the player bowls again. A ball is to be declared dead when any one of the following occurs:

—A player bowls on the wrong lane or out of turn.

—A player is interfered with by another bowler, a spectator, or a moving object.

—A pin or pins is missing from the setup, or is seen to move.

—The player's ball comes in contact with a foreign object.

NO PINS CONCEDED

One player is not allowed to concede pins to another. Only those pins actually knocked down or moved entirely off the playing surface of the lane as a result of a legal delivery may be counted.

BROKEN PINS

Should a pin or pins become broken or otherwise badly damaged during a game, it must be replaced immediately by another pin as uniform as possible in weight and condition with the set of pins being used. A broken pin does not affect the score made by a bowler.

BOWLING ON THE WRONG LANE

In league play, when a player bowls on the wrong lane (and the error is discovered before another player bowls), a dead ball shall be declared and the player required to bowl again on the correct lane.

BALLS, PERSONAL OWNERSHIP

A bowling ball used in a game and marked by its owner is considered personal property. Other participants in the game are prohibited from using it without the owner's consent.

FOULS

A foul is committed when a part of the bowler's person encroaches upon or goes beyond the foul line and touches any part of the lane, equipment, or building during or after the execution of a legal delivery. When a foul is committed no pinfall can be credited to the bowler, although the ball counts as a ball rolled.

Deliberate fouls are not allowed. If a player deliberately fouls to benefit by the calling of a foul, he shall be immediately disqualified from further participation in the series in play.

Fouling leads to these scoring situations:

—When a player fouls with the first ball of a frame, all the pins knocked down must be reset. Only those pins felled by the second ball are to be counted. Should the player knock down all the pins with his second ball, it shall be scored a spare. Should the player topple less than ten pins with his second ball, it is to be scored a miss.

—When a player fouls with his second ball of the frame, he receives credit only for those pins knocked down with his first ball.

—When a player fouls on both his first and second ball of a frame, he is not to be credited with any pins.

When a protest arises involving a foul or the legality of pinfall, and the protest cannot be resolved between the two team captains, a provisional ball or frame shall be bowled by the contestant.

Unreasonable Delay

League or tournament officials shall not permit any unreasonable delay in the progress of a game. Should any member or team participating in a league or tournament refuse to proceed with the game after being directed to do so by the proper authorities, the game or series shall be declared to be forfeited.

Judging Fouls

League or tournament officials shall select a foul judge. It shall be his duty to determine whether any of the players violate any of the provisions of the rules and regulations which pertain to fouls. League and tournament officials may also use any automatic foul-detecting device that has been granted ABC approval. Should the automatic foul-detecting device become temporarily inoperative, the tournament management shall assign official scorers to call fouls; in league play opposing captains are to act as foul judges. The failure to have automatic foul detectors in operation or to provide persons to act as foul judges shall disqualify the scores bowled from consideration for ABC high score awards.

Averages

A bowler's average is determined by dividing the total number of pins felled by the number of games bowled in one game in one season.

A composite average is the average pinfall for all leagues in which a player bowls. It is determined by adding the total number of pins felled in all leagues, and dividing the result by the total number of games.

Unfair Tactics

A bowler may be refused membership in the American Bowling Congress, or a current member may liable himself to suspension, for attempting to gain an unfair advantage. These tactics are to be regarded as improper:

—Directly or indirectly tampering with the lanes, bowling pins, or bowling balls.

—Misrepresenting an average in an effort to gain a larger handicap, or to qualify for a lower classification in a league or tournament.

—Establishing an average below one's ability in an effort to gain advantage in handicap or classified league or tournament competition.

Suspensions

A bowler's membership in the American Bowling Congress may be suspended should he fail to pay fees due for participation in a sanctioned league or tournament, or should he fail to distribute team prize money in accordance with verbal or written agreements. A suspended bowler is prohibited from competing with any team in a sanctioned league or tournament. Any team which grants membership to a suspended bowler shall forfeit all games in which said bowler participates, and the team may be suspended from membership in the American Bowling Congress.

Eligibility

A person who bowls in an unsanctioned league, or under an assumed name, or under the name of another tournament entrant, liables himself to suspension from the American Bowling Congress.

Fund Shortages

When an officer of a sanctioned league, or a chartered local or state association embezzles or absconds with funds entrusted to him, he shall be liable for indefinite suspension from the American Bowling Congress. The officer required to make monthly verifications of the accounts of said league or association, if found to be guilty of malfeasance or non-feasance, may also be liable for indefinite suspension of membership.

Protests

Any protest concerning league eligibility or general playing rules must be confirmed in writing to a responsible league or local association official of the American Bowling Congress within fifteen days after the alleged infraction takes place. If no written protest is entered within the fifteen-day period, the series must stand as bowled. Any protest concerning tournament eligibility or general playing rules must be filed within seventy-two hours.

Gambling

No bowling proprietor shall allow on his premises hand-books, pools, or any schemes of a gambling nature to be made involving the outcome of bowling games, whether the games be in league or tournament play.

Members of the American Bowling Congress may not participate in or operate any pool, lottery, or gambling scheme wherein the scores bowled in league or tournament play are used to determine the prize winners. No member of the ABC shall pay a supplemental fee of any type for the purpose of having a league or tournament score or scores qualify for prizes outside the league or tournament in which the score was bowled, except for charity purposes as provided below. The penalty for violation of this rule shall be suspension from ABC membership for both the participants and promoters.

Scores bowled in league play may be used to determine prize winners in a supplementary contest when the following conditions are observed:

—A minimum of two-thirds of the gross collected as entry fees is donated to a recognized charitable organization.

—Entry must be open to all bowlers in the local association and its metropolitan area.

—The entry fee must not exceed two dollars per person.

—Operating costs must not exceed ten cents per person.

—The local association under whose jurisdiction the event is held shall be represented officially on the managing or operating committee.

—The executive committee of the local association shall be authorized to withhold approval of the conditions herein described when the organization involved is determined not to be a bona fide charitable organization.

CARE OF APPROACHES

No one shall mark on or shall introduce on any part of the approach or lane any substance which will injure, disfigure, or place the approach or lane in such condition as to detract from the possibility of other bowlers being able to take advantage of the usual conditions. The use of such substances as aristol, talcum powder, pumice, or resin to alter the normal condition of the approach is strictly prohibited. The use of such substances on one's shoes, or the use of shoes with soft rubber heels or soles is also prohibited.

SCORING DEVICES

Any automatic scoring device approved by the ABC Board of Directors may be used in sanctioned league or tournament play. This device shall provide a printed record of the score and otherwise comply with the scoring and playing rules of the game.